DONATED BY
HARVARD UNIVERSITY'S
OFFICE OF
COMMUNITY AFFAIRS

IN HONOR OF

NEIL L. RUDENSTINE,
HARVARD'S 26TH PRESIDENT

JUNE 16, 2001

BOSTON PUBLIC LIBRARY

Victorian England

Titles in the World History Series

WORLD HISTORY SERIES

Victorian England

by
Clarice Swisher

Lucent Books, P.O. Box 289011, San Diego, CA 92198-9011

On Cover: View of the St. Pancras area of London, 1880's.

For Andrew

Library of Congress Cataloging-in-Publication Data

Swisher, Clarice, 1933–
  Victorian England / by Clarice Swisher.
      p. cm.—(World history series)
Includes bibliographical references (p.) and index.
Summary: Discusses Victorian England including the
transformation of a society, the Queen and her role; England at
the beginning of Victoria's reign; the impact of industrialization
and population growth on country and city; poverty, protests,
and politicians; the rise of the middle class; political, social, and
educational reforms; the importance of science, and England at
the end of the era.
  ISBN 1-56006-323-8 (alk. paper)
  1. Great Britain—History—Victoria, 1837-1901—Juvenile
literature. 2. England—Civilization—19th century—Juvenile
literature. [1. Great Britain—History—Victoria, 1837–1901.] I.
Title. II. Series.
  DA550 .S95 2001
  941.081—dc21

                                                    00-009249

Contents

Foreword

Each year on the first day of school, nearly every history teacher faces the task of explaining why his or her students should study history. One logical answer to this question is that exploring what happened in our past explains how the things we often take for granted—our customs, ideas, and institutions—came to be. As statesman and historian Winston Churchill put it, "Every nation or group of nations has its own tale to tell. Knowledge of the trials and struggles is necessary to all who would comprehend the problems, perils, challenges, and opportunities which confront us today." Thus, a study of history puts modern ideas and institutions in perspective. For example, though the founders of the United States were talented and creative thinkers, they clearly did not invent the concept of democracy. Instead, they adapted some democratic ideas that had originated in ancient Greece and with which the Romans, the British, and others had experimented. An exploration of these cultures, then, reveals their very real connection to us through institutions that continue to shape our daily lives.

Another reason often given for studying history is the idea that lessons exist in the past from which contemporary societies can benefit and learn. This idea, although controversial, has always been an intriguing one for historians. Those who agree that society can benefit from the past often quote philosopher George Santayana's famous statement, "Those who cannot remember the past are condemned to repeat it." Historians who subscribe to Santayana's philosophy believe that, for example, studying the events that led up to the major world wars or other significant historical events would allow society to chart a different and more favorable course in the future.

Just as difficult as convincing students to realize the importance of studying history is the search for useful and interesting supplementary materials that present historical events in a context that can be easily understood. The volumes in Lucent Books' World History Series attempt to present a broad, balanced, and penetrating view of the march of history. Ancient Egypt's important wars and rulers, for example, are presented against the rich and colorful backdrop of Egyptian religious, social, and cultural developments. The series engages the reader by enhancing historical events with these cultural contexts. For example, in Ancient Greece, the text covers the role of women in that society. Slavery is discussed in The Roman Empire, as well as how slaves earned their freedom. The numerous and varied aspects of everyday life in these and other societies are explored in each volume of the series. Additionally, the series covers the major political, cultural, and philosophical ideas as the torch of civilization is passed from ancient Mesopotamia and Egypt, through Greece, Rome, Medieval Europe, and other world cultures, to the modern day.

The material in the series is formatted in a thorough, precise, and organized manner. Each volume offers the reader a comprehensive and clearly written overview of an important historical event or period. The topic under discussion is placed in a broad, historical context. For example, The Italian Renaissance begins with a discussion of the High Middle Ages and the loss of central control that allowed certain Italian cities to develop artistically. The book ends by looking forward to the Reformation and interpreting the societal changes that grew out of the Renaissance. Thus, students are not only involved in an historical era, but also enveloped by the events leading up to that era and the events following it.

One important and unique feature in the World History Series is the primary and secondary source quotations that richly supplement each volume. These quotes are useful in a number of ways. First, they allow students access to sources they would not normally be exposed to because of the difficulty and obscurity of the original source. The quotations range from interesting anecdotes to farsighted cultural perspectives and are drawn from historical witnesses both past and present. Second, the quotes demonstrate how and where historians themselves derive their information on the past as they strive to reach a consensus on historical events. Lastly, all of the quotes are footnoted, familiarizing students with the citation process and allowing them to verify quotes and/or look up the original source if the quote piques their interest.

Finally, the books in the World History Series provide a detailed launching point for further research. Each book contains a bibliography specifically geared toward student research. A second, annotated bibliography introduces students to all the sources the author consulted when compiling the book. A chronology of important dates gives students an overview, at a glance, of the topic covered. Where applicable, a glossary of terms is included.

In short, the series is designed not only to acquaint readers with the basics of history, but also to make them aware that their lives are a part of an ongoing human saga. Perhaps they will then come to the same realization as famed historian Arnold Toynbee. In his monumental work, A Study of History, he wrote about becoming aware of history flowing through him in a mighty current, and of his own life "welling like a wave in the flow of this vast tide."

IMPORTANT DATES IN THE HISTORY OF VICTORIAN ENGLAND

1830
William IV ascends throne; Charles Lyell publishes *Principles of Geology;* rioting by workers; election of Charles Grey, a Whig.

1833
Factory Act is passed to protect children from being overworked.

1840
Annexation of New Zealand; Queen Victoria marries Prince Albert.

1842
Mine Act keeps women and young children from underground mines; anesthesia first used in surgery in America; Manchester-to-London railway opens.

1843
First telegraph line begins operation.

1846
Temporary repeal of Corn Laws, made permanent in 1848

1848
Public Health Act addresses urban sewage and water problems.

1830	1835	1840	1845	1850	1855

1832
First Reform Bill gives some middle-class men the right to vote.

1834
New Poor Law sends the poor to workhouses; establishment of London University.

1837
King William IV dies; his niece Victoria ascends the throne.

1838
First railroad train enters London.

1839
Chartist riots rage over social and economic conditions.

1844
Children's Factory Act restricts work hours for women and children.

1851
The Great Exhibition begins at Crystal Palace.

1854
Construction of London subway begins.

1870
Education Act makes elementary education available to all children; Charles Dickens dies.

1871
Abolition of religious qualification test at universities; trade unions legalized.

1884
Third Reform Bill equalizes electoral districts and enfranchises almost all adult males.

1869
Imprisonment for debt abolished.

1872
Ballot Act ensures secrecy in voting; first women admitted unofficially to Cambridge University examinations.

1888
County Councils Act; "Jack the Ripper" murders five women in London.

1867
Second Reform Bill allows more individuals the right to vote.

1860	1870	1880	1885	1890	1895

1861
Prince Albert dies of typhoid.

1879
First telephone exchange opens in London.

1897
Victoria's Diamond Jubilee.

1859
Charles Darwin publishes *On the Origin of Species.*

1901
Queen Victoria dies; her eldest son becomes King Edward VIII.

1878
Electric lights installed on some London streets; economic depression.

1858
Removal of property qualification for House of Commons.

The Transformation of a Society

During one of the most important periods in English history, there was a queen named Victoria, and her name has come to symbolize an entire era. This queen's reign lasted sixty-four years, from June 1837 until her death in January 1901, but many historians consider that the Victorian era began shortly before her birth and extended beyond her lifetime. Indeed, historian Anthony Wood says, "Victorianism, in some ways, preceded Victoria."[1] Some suggest that the Victorian era began with the coming of the railroad, which opened in 1824, and lasted until 1914, with the outbreak of World War I. In fact, the Victorian period in English history is defined not just by the monarch's reign, significant as it was, but by a number of sweeping changes in the society, economy, and culture of the British Empire.

The overriding theme of the Victorian period is change—economic, technological, social, and cultural. In 1831, six years before Victoria became queen, philosopher and author John Stuart Mill said "mankind have outgrown old institutions and old doctrines, and have not yet acquired new

ones."[2] During this period of shedding old institutions and searching for new ones, most of England's male citizens received the right to vote, the population doubled, the base of society changed from agriculture to industry, and Britain built a global empire with global markets. As Mill pointed out, there were no rules to help Britons of Victoria's day cope with these changes. It would be up to the Victorians to make the rules as they went along and, in the process, remake society.

The English were helped in their task by their spirit of confidence. The Victorians had confidence in themselves and in their country, confidence that they could succeed in their endeavors, and confidence that they could right themselves when they made mistakes. With rational-minded optimism, they believed that practical measures and practical solutions would lead them to success. At times such optimism blinded them to reality. Historians Hilary and Mary Evans describe this mindset: "The Victorians created, for their own amusement, a fantasy version of their own world. . . . Even [novelist] Charles

Dickens, for all his awareness of the bitter realities of Victorian life, was sufficiently a child of his age to be trapped into reinforcing its sentimental self-portrait."[3]

As part of this fantasy, middle-class Victorians wanted wealth and material possessions and believed that being rich was a sign of good character. Thus, they were willing to invest much energy in the acquisition of money and goods. Men, Victorians believed, achieved wealth from individual enterprise and hard work—with the result that the middle class came to see work as an end in itself. "Blessed is he who has found his work," essayist Thomas Carlyle wrote in *Past and Present*. "Let him ask no other blessedness."[4] In turn, morality was the key to enabling people to work long enough and hard enough to accumulate material wealth: If one was sufficiently sober, thrifty, and pious, rewards were bound to follow. And so it was these values that the middle-class Victorians tried to impose on themselves and their fellow countrymen.

This social revolution was embedded in the industrial revolution, which England pioneered. As a result of England's success, the Victorians showed the rest of the world how a society could manage

London, England, during the Victorian era, a time characterized by revolutionary changes in all areas of English society.

such drastic change while extending the advantages of democracy to give substantial numbers of citizens a voice in their own destiny. Through trial and error, the Victorians learned how to make crowded cities livable, and worked to build a humane society. They showed the rest of Europe and the young United States how to develop global markets and a manufacturing economy that raised the standard of living for nearly all citizens.

Although along the way farmers and workers suffered, intellectuals protested, and leaders modified their ideas, at least partly in response to the threat of violence, the country did not succumb to revolution. As the monarch presiding over this important period of transition, Queen Victoria is often seen as its focal point, although the question remains whether Queen Victoria defined the era or the era defined Victoria.

1 The Queen and Her Role

Victoria was born on May 24, 1819, the only child of Edward, duke of Kent, and German-born Victoria of Saxe-Coburg, who had been a princess in her native country. Edward died when Victoria was eight months old, and the little girl was reared by her mother, with the help of her loving governess Louise Lehzen. As Victoria matured, her uncle, Leopold, king of Belgium, served as a caring mentor and confidant.

Victoria's childhood was a sheltered one. Her mother was excessively protective of the fatherless child and kept her daughter close to her. Until Victoria became queen, the two slept in the same bedroom. Except for occasional visits to the country, Victoria saw little of the outside world and had no regular friends her own age other than cousins who occasionally visited. As a teenager she began keeping a daily diary to express her opinions and feelings. Taught by a tutor, Victoria mastered French, German, and English easily and studied the subjects usually taught to girls in aristocratic families of the time—singing, dancing, and sketching. To supplement her formal education, Victoria read history on her own, but for the remainder of her life, she regretted that she had no education in science.

In spite of her limited childhood world, Victoria developed a warm and thoughtful personality. Influenced in part by the books she read, Victoria became a simple, direct, and honest person. Her diary reveals the qualities she admired. Biographer and historian Dorothy Marshall reports:

> Directness and simplicity were qualities which she valued in other people's books. *The Exposition of the Gospel of St Matthew* by the Bishop of Chester she thought 'a very fine book indeed', adding 'Just the sort of book I like: which is just plain and comprehensible and full of truths and good feeling'. Her liking for similar qualities in human beings appears again and again. She commended her singing master Lablache, as 'a most good humoured, pleasing, agreeable and honest man'. Her cousin Ferdinand talked 'so clearly and so sensibly', and on further acquaintance she wrote that she found him 'so sensible, so natural, so unaffected, and unsophisticated and so *truly* good'.[5]

Clearly, Victoria had strong emotions, and she often expressed them. Her diary reveals her tenderhearted nature by her repeated use of the word "dear" to express her appreciation for people she liked. On the other hand, she could be temperamental and stubborn, erupting in nervous displays and angry outbursts. These traits and behaviors she exhibited throughout her life.

Like many nineteenth-century English females, Victoria felt most comfortable when she had a strong man to depend on. Her uncle, King Leopold, saw the likelihood that she would follow another uncle, William IV, as monarch, and tried to groom her from an early age to act and think like a queen.

VICTORIA BECOMES QUEEN

Victoria was only eighteen years old when on June 20, 1837, William IV died, and the young princess was awakened during the night to learn that she was the queen of England. She had been envisioning herself in the role of queen and knew she could call on Leopold for advice. At the beginning of her reign, Victoria assumed firm control.

Dorothy Marshall sets the scene: "Her dignity and self-possession, in spite of her small stature—Victoria was only five foot two inches—surprised and delighted her

Eighteen-year-old Victoria somberly accepts the news of her accession to the throne of England.

Queen Victoria receives the sacrament in a religious ceremony following her coronation. Victoria was crowned on June 28, 1838, in London's Westminster Abbey.

ministers and her Privy Council [appointees who act in an advisory and judicial capacity]."[6] Lord Melbourne, prime minister at the time, became the young queen's trusted adviser and close friend. Melbourne was "very much a man of the world, well-informed, witty, endowed with great charm, a beautiful speaking voice and an uninhibited laugh."[7] Victoria, who liked Melbourne and admired his strength, found in him a father figure, and he, being attentive and protective, treated her like a daughter. Thus, with her own capabilities and a good adviser, Victoria's unofficial reign had a strong beginning.

The official coronation, on June 28, 1838, came a month after Victoria's nineteenth birthday. Crowds thronged the streets to watch the procession from Buckingham Palace to Westminster Abbey, the traditional location of British coronations. It was during the coronation that an unanticipated incident revealed Victoria's warmth and enshrined the new queen in the hearts of her subjects. After an old man stumbled twice on the steps as he moved to kiss the queen's hand, she left her throne, went to the head of the steps, and offered her hand.

Despite her obvious kindness, Victoria soon proved she could be tough, though it was a minor incident on which she made her stand. Lord Melbourne's political opponents, the Tories, wielded their parliamentary strength to select Sir Robert Peel as prime minister. Peel asked Victoria to replace members of her staff who were, like

Victoria Marries Prince Albert

Although Victoria had clearly established herself as Britain's monarch, Leopold and others believed she should have a husband. Finding a suitable mate, however, required some finesse. A husband for a reigning queen must be not only a man of proper lineage but also one who will accept his wife's legal position as ruler. King Leopold suggested Victoria's first cousin, Prince Albert of Saxe-Coburg-Gotha. Victoria liked the idea. A handsome and intelligent man, Albert had studied science, philosophy, political economy, painting, and music. Moreover, he was a good man: "kind, gentle, patient, and loyal. . . . 'Albert is beautiful,'"[9] Victoria wrote in her journal when he visited her. Since court etiquette prevents a man from proposing to a queen, Victoria had to initiate the proposal. Marshall reports that the young queen found the courage to tell her cousin that it would make her "too happy" if he would consent to marry her. Later Victoria wrote in her journal that Albert's first embrace was the "brightest, happiest moment"[10] of her life.

Victoria's cousin and husband, Prince Albert of Saxe-Coburg-Gotha.

Melbourne, Whigs and to accept a new Tory staff, but she refused, arguing that she would not dismiss her loyal ladies-in-waiting. The cabinet of ministers sided with Victoria, and Peel was forced to back down and resign; Melbourne remained the prime minister for another two years. Marshall concludes: "This determined young woman had got both Lord Melbourne and Sir Robert Peel where she wanted them. . . . She had fought her campaign with tenacity and skill. . . . Whatever the case, it was no mean achievement, and indicative of her toughness, loyalty and sheer cleverness when fighting for a cause in which she believed."[8]

Albert's Public and Private Roles

Victoria and Albert were married on February 10, 1840, in the Chapel Royal, St. James's Palace. After Victoria married Albert, he became the master of the house, moral guide, and the man upon whom Victoria depended. He served as

ALBERT'S CONTRIBUTIONS TO SOCIETY

In "Albert, Prince Consort," historian Tamie Watters highlights Albert's contributions to English politics and culture, contributions more significant than those of the queen. Watters's essay is published in Sally Mitchell's Victorian Britain: An Encyclopedia.

As Victoria's advisor and private secretary, he impressed successive prime ministers, even cocksure Lord Palmerston, with his foresight. . . . Just before he died in 1861 of overwork and fever, he probably prevented war with America by softening Lord John Russell's inflammatory letter to Washington over a federal warship boarding the British *Trent.*

Albert helped stabilize the British monarchy when midcentury revolutions were sweeping away crowned heads in Europe. His uprightness and family life set standards for the nation. He cultivated artists and men of learning, had Mendelssohn perform at court, and enriched the royal collection with medieval and early Renaissance art. Periodic suspicions of his national loyalty wounded him, and he was not the unbending German often portrayed but a lover of fun, a good mimic, . . . and a devoted father.

Albert and Victoria at the time of their marriage.

her private secretary and confidential adviser on all public matters; he drafted numerous memoranda in her name and chaired committees for the arts, sciences, industry, agriculture, and even the army.

Although Victoria loved Albert whole-heartedly, the British public initially failed to share her enthusiasm. His German nationality made him unpopular with many of Victoria's subjects, who questioned his loyalty to Britain. Albert worked hard at winning his new countrymen's acceptance. One major project, the Great Exhibition of 1851, the culmination of Albert's vision and his hard work on the committees that oversaw the arts, sciences, and industry, was what finally won the British over. A historian notes that the immensely popular Exhibition was unprecedented:

> The enormous Crystal Palace, with its canopy of glass and steel built over and around the trees in Hyde Park, and occupying a site of twenty-six acres, combined engineering utility and beauty in one staggering whole. It is difficult today, when towering skyscrapers are commonplace, to realise

The spectacular Crystal Palace, site of the Great Exhibition of 1851. People from all over Britain flocked to the Crystal Palace to view the exhibits and the building itself.

VICTORIA MOURNS THE LOSS OF HER HUSBAND

Dorothy Thompson sheds light on Victoria's seclusion with commentary on Victoria's self-centeredness and her passion. The excerpt comes from Queen Victoria: The Woman, the Monarch, and the People.

After her husband's death the queen clearly became more self-absorbed and self-centered. She withdrew from many of the public functions of the monarch, and viewed with some ambivalence those which she still fulfilled. In her private and personal life she encountered on a more exalted scale the problems faced by many Victorian 'relics' [widows].

The loss of her husband was a physical as well as a social and spiritual loss. She wrote in her journal, 'What a dreadful going to bed! What a contrast to that tender lover's love! All alone!' She had always had a strongly passionate nature. In a letter written a few months before Albert's death she had declared, 'My nature is too passionate, my emotions too fervent, and I am a person who has to cling to some one in order to find peace and comfort.'

---

the daring of the conception, based on the glass-houses at Chatsworth. The effect was tremendous not only on the people of London, but on people of Britain, not only on the middle classes— whose temple it was—but also on the workers everywhere. They came in their thousands: excursion trains were run from the provinces to bring workers from the industrial towns. Many Londoners visited the Exhibition again and again.[11]

To the Crystal Palace came 6 million visitors eager to see machines and instruments they had only heard of. The profits from the exhibit helped to fund two great public buildings, Albert Hall and the Victoria and Albert Museum. In 1859 Albert's important contributions were recognized when he was given the official title of prince consort.

SORROW AND DEATH

Victoria's marriage to Albert was not merely a political arrangement. The couple had nine children. For twenty years, the royal family, like other British families, enjoyed such simple pleasures as ice skating and reading together, and Victoria and Albert accepted many of the usual burdens and responsibilities of their children's upbringing.

Unfortunately, Victoria's happiness was not to last, and 1861 was the darkest year in her life. In December of that year, Albert, exhausted from overwork, contracted typhoid fever. Within two weeks he was dead, leaving Victoria a widow at forty-two. Biographer Marshall notes that Albert's death was a tremendous blow: "For twenty years they had been apart for hardly more than a few days. In every crisis both domestic and public he had always been behind her. Now she was left with a void so deep and so black that the mere contemplation of it drove her to the verge of despair."[12] England too suffered the loss of a gracious public servant. Conservative Tory leader Benjamin Disraeli offered Albert a special tribute, lavishly praising the "wisdom and energy" with which "this German prince"[13] had served England.

But losing her husband was not the only grief Victoria had to endure. She had earlier lost her mother, with whom she had reconciled after years of ill feeling. She had also experienced the embarrassment of a family sex scandal when her son Leopold's affair with an actress, Nellie Clifton, became public knowledge. This incident particularly appalled the queen, who had personally adopted Albert's strict moral standards and had resolved to be moral leader of the nation.

VICTORIA WITHDRAWS

In the aftermath of a year of sadness and death, Queen Victoria withdrew from public view. She spent little time in her London home, Buckingham Palace, instead favoring more remote residences such as Windsor Castle, the winter palace Osborne House on the Isle of Wight, and Balmoral in the Scottish Highlands. Ministers traveled to these imposing venues to deliver reports and hear the queen's thoughts, which she was determined would be a continuation of Albert's ideas. As she said, "His *wishes, his* plans . . . about *every*thing, his views about every thing are to be *my laws!* And no human *power* will make me swerve from what *he* decided and wished."[14]

Always extremely emotional, Victoria now embodied loss. Once when Albert had been briefly absent, she had revealed to an aide, "I feel very lonely without my dear Master; and though I know other people are often separated for a few days I feel habit could not get me accustomed to it."[15] After Albert's death her feelings of loneliness and loss intensified to a point of desperation. Her therapy was to go to her husband's big granite tomb, topped with a marble figure of Albert; there she gazed on his face and knelt in prayer. For several years she sought to maintain her grief-stricken seclusion.

The shock of Albert's death had so devastated Victoria that she experienced what modern observers would term a long, deep depression. During this period, she developed a close, dependent relationship with a Scottish servant, John Brown, who frequently was seen at the queen's side in public. Although it is

The Enigma of Victoria's Relationship with Brown

Victoria's relationship with John Brown was an enigma to her contemporaries and still puzzles modern historians in that it manifests contradictions between the queen's values and her behavior, here clarified by Dorothy Thompson in Victoria: The Woman, the Monarch, and the People.

What is surprising is not the fact of the John Brown relationship itself, clear and undeniable as it was, but the extent to which she was prepared, for the sake of it, to go against so much of what seemed to be her nature and her beliefs. For the whole John Brown episode deeply offended her children, upset and alienated some of her closest retainers and servants, caused gossip and ribaldry among those of the general public and press who took note of it and clearly worried her court and political advisers. Victoria had a strong sense of public duty and the highest possible regard for the dignity of her office. She was also strongly convinced of the need to observe the class divisions in the society of her time. Nevertheless, the evidence is overwhelming that these considerations did not prevent her from contracting a relationship with a man who was of humble birth and was by occupation a servant, a relationship closer and more intimate than she had with any other man after her husband's death.

Queen Victoria and John Brown at Balmoral, the queen's residence in the Scottish Highlands.

highly unlikely that Victoria and Brown had a physical relationship, any suggestion of intimacy horrified the British people. Thus the combination of Victoria's "dates" with Brown and her lengthy neglect of her duties sparked criticism in the newspapers and great consternation among the population at large.

The Queen Resumes Her Duties

Victoria weathered the public disapproval in silence, showing little awareness of the distress her relationship with John Brown was causing. As the tenth anniversary of Albert's death approached, however, the queen was abruptly jolted out of her personal misery: Her son Edward, the Prince of Wales, became very ill with typhoid fever. She left Balmoral and went to Windsor to be near him. Victoria was certain she would lose her eldest son to the same disease that had killed her husband. The whole country worried with the queen. The situation looked grim as the prince's condition remained serious through the Christmas holidays; then, surprisingly, in January his condition improved and he made a full recovery. On February 27, 1872, Victoria and Edward attended a public service of thanksgiving at St. Paul's Cathedral, commemorating the prince's return to health and signifying the return of the queen to public life. From then on Victoria played her part in the affairs of the nation.

Victoria returned to public life, but she delegated the affairs of state to Benjamin Disraeli, now prime minister, with whom she felt in accord. Instead of participating in discussions of the details of government policy, Victoria confined her attention to family events and public appearances, such as the weddings of her children, which she celebrated with warmth and elegance.

By the time England celebrated the sixtieth anniversary of Queen Victoria's reign in 1897, the British Empire was at the height of its power and prestige. The people were enthusiastic about Britain's imperial designs as they had not been since Victoria came to the throne. Historians Sally Mitchell and James D. Startt explain:

> At the end of the nineteenth century the British Empire covered one-fourth of the earth's land and included a quarter of its population. . . . In addition, the British dominated international shipping and communications, provided the capital and engineering for rail networks on every continent,

Queen Victoria in 1897, the year of her Diamond Jubilee.

and recreated a distinctive pattern of life and values wherever they settled. In early Victorian times the empire had little meaning for most Britons, but by the century's closing decades the country was swept by a wave of "new imperialism" that climaxed with Queen Victoria's Diamond Jubilee in 1897. British superiority seemed unassailable and unquestionable.[16]

The queen attended many of the public events scheduled for her Diamond Jubilee, though she was seventy-eight years old and in frail health. At Buckingham Palace she received her many guests from a wheelchair. She rode in the procession to Westminster Abbey in her landau drawn by eight cream-colored horses and responded to the cheering crowds along the way, although the service of thanksgiving at Westminster was shortened in deference to her age.

Following the service, the queen returned to Buckingham Palace. There, in a ceremony that symbolized British technological prowess, she pressed an electric button that sent a telegram throughout the empire. It read: "From my heart I thank my beloved people. May God bless them."[17]

In the year after the Diamond Jubilee the queen, saddened by the death of friends and limited by failing eyesight and rheumatism, made fewer public appearances. Still, Victoria made an effort to fulfill her obligations as monarch, making an extended trip to Ireland, a duty she had neglected since Albert's death. And mindful of her ability to raise the morale of her subjects, she paid occasional calls on institutions that served the people, such as hospitals for wounded soldiers.

Victoria struggled on heroically until the end of 1900, when her New Year's Day diary account lamented that she felt weak and unwell. Her diary, which she had kept religiously since she was thirteen, stopped after January 13. On January 19 the message went out that the queen was in poor health. Three days later, on January 22, surrounded by her children and grandchildren, Queen Victoria died. In accord with her instructions, her coffin was borne on a gun carriage to the place where Albert was buried. Her body was placed next to Albert's, in an identical mausoleum.

By the time Victoria died, she had become an icon, known and loved more for her long reign, her memorable public appearances, and her personal dignity than for any policies she had effected or causes she had supported. The abilities to survive many sorrows and to adapt to the incredible changes of the nineteenth century reflect the strength and flexibility deliberately cultivated by this remarkable woman. England at the time of Victoria's death was a very different place from England at the time of her coronation.

Chapter

2 England at the Beginning of Victoria's Reign

When Victoria was crowned queen in 1837, English society was structured much as it had been for hundreds of years. England had built an empire of colonies around the world, and the people at home lived in a society organized along strict class lines, centered around an agri-

VICTORIAN ENGLAND

cultural economy and a hereditary system of nobility. In this agrarian way of life, the upper classes controlled both the land and the government. As Victoria began her reign, however, the industrial revolution, which was already under way, was beginning to have major effects on established institutions.

THE BRITISH EMPIRE

England had built an empire by starting trading companies around the world and then expanding them into colonies. First the trading companies acquired raw materials not available in England and found markets for export products. As the companies grew and prospered, settlers seeking opportunities not directly related to foreign trade moved into the areas. These settlements, in turn, became colonies, the first of which were the North American colonies, which the British Empire lost in the Revolutionary War of 1776. After struggles with French commercial and colonial interests, England came to dominate India in 1757 and won control of Canada in 1763. The 1769 voyage of the famous explorer Captain James Cook paved the way to bring Australia into the British Empire, and the first group of English convicts from crowded English prisons followed Cook's voyage as settlers in Sydney in 1788. New Zealand became a colony when English convicts, having escaped from Australia, settled there. After a conflict with the Dutch, England acquired the Union of South Africa in 1806. Besides these major colonies, England gained control in Burma (now Myanmar), Ceylon (now Sri Lanka), Malaya (now Malaysia), Singapore, and Hong Kong. When Victoria became queen, this empire stretched across the globe.

By the beginning of Victoria's reign, the English had learned how to manage an empire. Maintaining colonies required many kinds of workers. Adventurous Englishmen took advantage of opportunities to go to colonies to make money as traders, planters of crops, or administrators. Some returned home, but some stayed permanently. In the early part of the Victorian period overpopulation and poverty in England caused many people to immigrate to colonies. Because the English people felt that they had a superior culture, many went to the colonies with the idea of spreading Christianity, English customs, and the English language. In 1823 the founder of Singapore, Sir T. Stamford Raffles, wrote to a friend in the East India Company telling of his work in Singapore. This passage also illustrates the attitude of cultural superiority that typified British imperialism in the Victorian era:

CONFLICT CAUSED BY COLONIZATION

Historian Paul Kennedy, in The Rise and Fall of Great Powers, *reports that expensive colonial acquisitions evoked opposition from many commentators on behalf of taxpayers. Kennedy describes the extraordinary expansion of the British Empire in a fifty-year period.*

"Yet whatever rhetoric of anti-imperialism within Britain, the fact was that the empire continued to grow, expanding (according to one calculation) at an average annual pace of about 100,000 square miles between 1815 and 1865. Some were strategical/commercial acquisitions, like Singapore, Aden, the Falkland Islands, Hong Kong, Lagos; others were the consequence of land-hungry white settlers, moving across the South African veldt, the Canadian prairies, and the Australian outback—whose expansion usually provoked a native resistance that often had to be suppressed by troops from Britain or British India. And even when formal annexations were resisted by a home government perturbed at this growing list of responsibilities, the 'informal influence' of expanding British society was felt from Uruguay to the Levant and from the Congo to the Yangtze."

Schools have been set on foot on a very respectable scale, and I trust these moral and religious institutions will be a sufficient counterpoise for the commercial character of the People—and at any rate prevent them from becoming too exclusively commercial. . . . We shall require more aid from Europe—a dozen good and zealous missionaries would find abundant employment in extending the objects of the Institution. . . . At Bencoolen our Schools have succeeded admirable—the Parent School contains upwards of 200 Boys who are trained on the plan of the British and Foreign School Society—and if we do not advance the intellect we shall at any rate teach them discipline and good habits. If we have no great chance of mending the present generation, we may entertain hopes of doing something for the next.[18]

Clearly the empire was built with both economic and moral purposes. Because the enterprise required transportation to and from the colonies, England developed a large merchant navy equipped to move people and trading goods. Though all of these elements of the empire were established at the beginning of Victoria's reign, the empire continued to grow throughout the era.

THE CLASS STRUCTURE

Like the British Empire, the structure of English society was already firmly established at the beginning of the Victorian era. England was an agrarian society with distinct upper, middle, and lower classes, each of which comprised different levels of rank, different living conditions and manners, and different forms of social life.

Just beneath the royalty—the monarch and his or her family—was the aristocracy, the class that had governed England since the late 1500s. At the beginning of the Victorian period about three hundred aristocratic families were identifiable by ancestry, wealth, and family name. Beneath the aristocracy was the gentry, those who owned at least three hundred acres of land and were qualified to apply for a coat of arms and append the title of Esquire to their names. The gentry shared many of the privileges and beliefs of the aristocracy. There were five ranks of upper-class gentlemen who inherited the right to hold titles and sit in the parliamentary House of Lords. Besides titles, the aristocracy and the gentry shared the luxury of free time for public service because neither wealthy group had to work for money. At the lowest level of the upper class came the knights and the baronets, who were not permitted to sit in the House of Lords, but were permitted election to the House of Commons, the lower house of Parliament.

Beneath the aristocracy, the gentry, and the knights were merchants and shopkeepers; professional men such as lawyers, doctors, and teachers; military officers; and industrialists, a new breed altogether. At the beginning of Victoria's reign, the middle class had no political power, no rank, and little recognition. Later in the nineteenth century, however, this class vastly increased in numbers and influence.

At the bottom of the social ladder were tenant farmers, farm laborers, and uneducated city laborers, a group who had traditionally been called simply "the poor." In *Victorian People and Ideas,* historian Richard D. Altick identifies new labels for the so-called working class at the beginning of the Victorian period:

> Now it was "the masses," "the million," "the laboring poor," and, increasingly, "the people.". . . These were the laborers in the fields and factories, the unskilled and semi-skilled as well as the more expert in their occupations, who were a group apart, because their work was steadier.[19]

Within the lower class distinct differences were visible depending on workers' skills, circumstances, and determination to advance themselves and secure better lives for their children.

CLASSES WITHIN CLASSES

Each class had ranks within it and each was characterized by traditional kinds of work. In addition, each class encompassed different cultural and social practices. The aristocracy and gentry lived in the country in large castles surrounded by moats and many acres of fields and woods. Wives often managed these large

Wealthy English citizens enjoy a garden party. England's upper class consisted of the aristocracy, gentry, knights, and baronets.

estates because their husbands were occupied by public projects or political office. Altick explains:

> In earlier centuries, the families of great landed wealth and supreme social position had formed the oligarchy which whether behind the scenes or publicly in Parliament and offices of government, had determined the nation's course. They had also constituted a cultural leadership, which had been largely responsible for the flourishing of English civilization from the time of Elizabeth I to that of George III.[20]

These upper-class families observed strict standards of behavior and language and provided leadership in education, the arts, and culture. Historian Sidney Johnson reports that "an increasingly strict observance of precedence and etiquette differentiated the ranks of nobility from one another and from the monied professional and middle classes."[21] For recreation the upper classes entertained guests with elaborate dinner parties and balls. The primary activity for men was hunting on their own estates, especially the foxhunt, in which men on horseback and packs of trained hounds chased a fox across the countryside. Children of these families were trained in the etiquette and conventions of their class and educated by tutors. Boys were sent to exclusive private institutions, confusingly called public schools, to prepare them to attend university at Oxford or Cambridge.

The middle classes aspired to be like the upper classes though they had no opportunity to participate in governing their society. Middle-class success depended on education, wealth, and the ability to emulate the language and manners of the upper classes. Only a few advanced into elite circles. The rest lived in smaller houses surrounded by fewer acres, and participated in less elaborate parties and entertainments. Though they sought the same customs as the upper classes, they had to work for a living, and hence were constrained by limited means and time.

The working classes composed the largest segment of the population. In the agrarian society of pre-Victorian days, most average people worked on farms. Many tenant farmers rented land from upper-class estate owners, and with the help of the owners worked hard to improve the land and farm successfully. The majority of the men, women, and children, however, worked as agricultural laborers, farm servants, and shepherds. Altick describes their circumstances:

> Country laborers in every period were accustomed to living from hand to mouth. Their homes were hovels built of mud, lath, and plaster, with floors of dirt or stone, and rafters instead of ceiling under the leaky thatch. Domestic fowl and animals such as pigs shared these dark, damp, sparsely furnished quarters with the family. There was no sanitation, and often there was no adequate heat. It had been a hard, grim life, whose only purpose, year after year, was somehow to extract the bare essentials of diet and clothing from field and pasture. It was lightened only by

SOCIAL LIFE OF THE WELL-TO-DO

Upper-class Victorians living in rural villages enjoyed an active social life that included both outdoor and indoor functions. With wealth came leisure, and the village gentry proved adept at devising ways to entertain themselves. Freed from daily work, they arranged elaborate sporting events for men. One of the favorite activities was shooting parties to hunt deer and wild birds. The passion for hunting generated jobs for gameskeepers, who protected the game on the estates between hunts, and beaters, who scared up birds for the shooters during the actual events. Another favorite activity was the hunting party, an occasion that involved the whole community. All farmers who owned horses were allowed to ride. Servants cheered as the riders started out and returned. Laborers lined up to watch and shouted to the hounds on the fox's track. At the end of the hunt there was eating and celebration.

Although in those days women did not ride to the hounds, they participated in a crowded schedule of parties. Old diaries reveal that a favorite was tea served in late afternoon. Women of all generations dressed in their finest clothes and drank tea and ate delicate sweets using their finest manners. Balls, elaborate dinners, and parties engaged entire families in dancing and games. When large groups were invited, they gathered in the assembly rooms of the nearby market town. Many of these social events gave young men and women an opportunity to meet and to practice their manners.

Wealthy Victorians spent much of their time at parties and sporting events, such as horse racing.

the occasional holidays and fairs that punctuated the march of the seasons and by an oral folk culture of stories, songs, and superstitions.[22]

In this strict class society, the lower classes were locked into a way of life and had few opportunities to improve their status or to acquire the political power to change their lives or the lives of their children.

The upper classes, on the other hand, held considerable political power. The aristocracy and the gentry controlled both Parliament and local government offices. Moreover, custom and tradition supported the status quo, making change almost impossible in pre-nineteenth-century England. Historian David Hopkinson reports on one politician's concern about the class system in 1837 at Queen Victoria's accession:

> Benjamin Disraeli [who later would serve Victoria as prime minister] criticized a "mortgaged" aristocracy, a middle class only just struggling into existence, a peasantry too numerous to support itself, and a rootless urban working class which was economically and culturally degraded. A society so stratified was in desperate need of leadership and reform.[23]

THE INDUSTRIAL REVOLUTION

The process of reform that Disraeli called for was already under way as an unintended consequence of the industrial revolution. Beginning in the eighteenth century, the factory system transformed

Benjamin Disraeli, prime minister of England during Victoria's reign, advocated social reform.

work from manufacturing goods by hand to mass-producing manufactured goods in factories with large machines. The factory system underpinned the industrial revolution and gradually transformed society.

The industrial revolution was founded on two major inventions—the steam engine and the Bessemer process for making the steel required for the engines of trains, ships, and factory machinery. In 1769 James Watt patented an improved steam engine, without which the industrial revolution would have been much delayed if not impossible. The steam engine provided power for transportation and factory machines. The introduction of an efficient process for making steel from iron ore made possible the production of rails for railroads, engines for trains, machines for factories, and hulls and engines for steamships, all contributing to the demand for transportation and manufacture.

Another important element in the industrial revolution was the development of an efficient transportation system. A canal system was built to connect England's many rivers and waterways. This system provided a cheap method for moving heavy goods, such as iron for making steel and coal for running the steam engines. Then engineers Richard Trevithick and George Stephenson adapted the steam engine to power trains, and the English built a system of tracks to connect towns and cities. Historians T. Walter Wallbank and Alastair M. Taylor describe the first trains:

> In 1825 the first English railroad was opened, the famous Stockton and Darlington. The engine was driven by Stephenson himself at the dizzy speed of over four miles an hour. A signalman on horseback dashed in front to warn spectators of the approach of the iron monster, its chimney red-hot and belching forth clouds of smoke and sparks. But it was a real engine. Another line opened in 1830, this time from Liverpool to Manchester, and Stephenson's *Rocket* made what was then the terrifying speed of 29 miles an hour.[24]

Improvements in trains and a network of tracks resulted in much greater capacity for the transport of large volumes of raw materials and finished products alike. By the time Victoria became queen, trains ran regularly between England's major cities on five hundred miles of track. The steam engine was next installed in ships, and by 1838 it was the sole source of power for ships crossing the Atlantic. Wallbank and Taylor note the significance of these technological developments: "Vast quantities of cotton, rubber, jute, copper, lumber, oils, and tin—and many other materials—had to be imported. This would not have been possible without the existence of cheap and efficient transportation."[25]

The steam power that underlay England's transportation system also provided the energy to manufacture goods

James Watt patented his steam engine in 1769, ushering in the industrial revolution.

SKEPTICAL REACTION TO THE NEW RAILWAY TRAINS

The first steam locomotives functioned crudely and offered passengers an uncomfortable ride. In The Victorian World Picture, *David Newsome describes early public reaction.*

"At first extreme scepticism was expressed at the possibility that passengers might be conveyed by an iron horse. The Stockton-Darlington Railway, engineered by [George] Stephenson, was opened in 1825, and an experimental passenger-coach trundled along it pulled by horses—otherwise, people said, how could you get it to stop, and what would happen going downhill without a drag? This was not quite such a foolish question as it might seem. When Stephenson won a prize for his high-speed 'Rocket' (it could travel at 28 miles per hour) and the Manchester-Liverpool line was opened for passenger use in 1830 by an extremely sceptical Duke of Wellington, tragedy occurred. As the Rocket stopped to take on water at Parkside, William Huskisson, MP [member of Parliament] for Liverpool, rashly disembarked, and panicked when he saw that the engine was still moving. He ran on to the line and was crushed to death.

This was an inauspicious start, but the railways had come to stay, and to expand at a fantastic rate, though the early arrangements for passenger conveyance were somewhat makeshift and even grotesque. Guards had to be posted on the outside of carriages to make sure that couplings did not disengage; sometimes they would lock the carriage doors in order to discourage the over-curious or those who might in panic try to alight when the train was in motion. Gentry were allowed to remain in their own private coaches, hoisted and fastened on to a flat truck. The journey itself could prove extremely uncomfortable. [Poet and biographer] Richard Monckton Milnes took his first trip by train in the summer of 1831, and described the experience to his mother:

> We went quick enough (36 miles in an hour and twenty minutes), but it made you so giddy to look on the ground, and the dust flew so disagreeably in your eyes, that unless one slept all the way, a long steam journey would be anything but pleasant. . . . I cannot conceive a possible accident if you only sit still, for if the boiler were to burst, it could not hurt those in the inside of the carriages. I believe a good many engineers are killed."

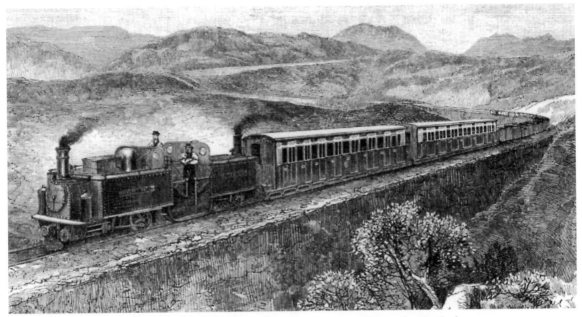

The manufacturing of trains increased during the Victorian era, when technological advances allowed for the efficient production of steel used for rails and engines.

in factories. By 1837 England had already opened several. Historian Wilson J. Hoffman defines the relatively new workplace: "A factory or mill is a centralized place of production under one roof, utilizing large-scale units of operation, laborsaving machinery, and regimented labor."[26] Large factories with long rows of workers sitting before identical machines first produced manufactured textiles beginning in 1770. Eventually, goods of all kinds were made in factories instead of being crafted by hand in small shops.

At the heart of the industrial revolution, even more important than an inexplicably rising population, was the factory system. Historian David Newsome observes:

> No section of society was untouched by the vast increase in population (it practically doubled between 1801 and 1851). . . . The most powerful impact of all, however, was the massive advance of technology and industrialization, which was visibly shaping both the landscape and the social structure of the whole country.[27]

3 The Impact of Industrialization and Population Growth on Country and City

Technological and industrial change and a rise in population accelerated during the early reign of Queen Victoria and had a profound effect on the countryside and the cities of England. Normally social change is gradual, but early Victorian England was an exception, at least in the minds of the citizens at that time. Historian David Newsome says:

> Nature does nothing by a jump, it is said. But to the British people living at the time, it seemed as if the world they knew had vanished almost overnight. Quite apart from the awesome revolution in transport . . . it was the suddenness of the changes that was the dominant note in the writings and reflections of contemporaries. Even the word "industry," in the sense understood today, was a novelty.[28]

Victorian essayist and poet Matthew Arnold worried that change was occurring in every aspect of life faster than society could assimilate it; such major changes as population growth and industrialization could, he thought, cause the society to become "overheated."[29]

POPULATION GROWTH

For reasons not entirely understood by contemporary or modern scholars, the population increased rapidly during the Victorian period and reached its highest rate of increase in the 1870s. In 1801 England had a population of nearly 11 million; by 1901 the population had risen to 37 million, an increase of 300 percent in a century. Marriages increased and family size grew until 1870, when the average family included five or six children, before tapering down to three or four children after 1870. Infant mortality remained the same, but life expectancy increased as health care improved. The population also grew because workers from Ireland and Scotland immigrated to find work, but at the same time many Englishmen emmigrated to Crown colonies like Hong Kong. For whatever combination of reasons, the country simply had an alarming number of people who needed jobs, food, and housing.

The population was not only increasing, but on the move from rural areas to cities. In early Victorian England, 75 percent of the people lived in rural towns and villages primarily in the southern part of the country; at the end of the era, 75 percent of the population lived in large cities, especially London and in the Midlands and the north, places that had been sparsely populated at the beginning of the Victorian era. London became the most urbanized city in Europe. Transportation, industry, and the rising population shift to cities changed the British landscape.

NEW FORMS OF TRANSPORTATION CHANGE THE ENGLISH LANDSCAPE

The new methods of transport demanded by the industrial revolution noticeably changed the British landscape. Canals formed waterways where none had been, built often by cutting into hills and filling valleys. By 1848 the countryside was crisscrossed by five thousand miles of iron track, and railway terminals and hotels replaced the inns where stagecoach travelers had lodged for the night. The railway builders dug tunnels and built viaducts and bridges, and the trains left trails of steam, smoke, and sparks. Victorian novelist William Thackeray writes that the railroad

> starts the new era, and we of a certain age belong to the new time and the old one. . . . We elderly people have

A large Victorian family gathers around the piano. England's family size peaked in 1870, when the average couple had five or six children.

Antagonism Toward the Coming Railways

Scottish author and biographer Samuel Smiles enumerates public objections to the coming railways. This excerpt from The Life of George Stephenson, Railway Engineer, *illustrates early-nineteenth-century British resistance to change. The author's prorailroad bias is clearly indicated by the contemptuous language he uses to describe the objections, many of which turned out to be valid.*

"Railways had thus, like most other great social improvements, to force their way against the fierce antagonism of united ignorance and prejudice. Public-spirited obstructives were ready to choke the invention at its birth, on the ground of the general good. The forcible invasion of property—the intrusion of public roads into private domains—the noise and nuisance caused by locomotives and the danger of fire to the adjoining property were dwelt upon *ad nauseam*. The lawlessness of navvies [construction and excavation laborers] was a source of great terror to quiet villages. Then the breed of horses would be destroyed; country innkeepers would be ruined; posting towns would become depopulated; turnpike roads would be deserted; and the institution of the English Stagecoach, with its rosy gilled coachman and guard, known to every buxom landlady at roadside country inns, would be destroyed for ever. Fox-covers and game-preserves would be interfered with; agricultural communication destroyed; land thrown out of cultivation; landowners and farmers alike reduced to beggary; the poor rates increased in consequence of the number of labourers thrown out of employment by the railroads; and all this in order that Liverpool, Manchester, and Birmingham manufacturers, merchants, and cotton-spinners might establish a monstrous monopoly in railroads! However, there was always this consolation to wind up with,—that the canals would beat the railroads, and that, even when the latter were made, the public would not use them, nor trust either their persons or their goods to the risks of railway accidents and explosions. They would thus prove only monuments of the folly of their projectors, whom they must inevitably involve in ruin and disaster."

lived in that prae [pre]-railroad world, which has passed into limbo and vanished from under us. I tell you it was firm under our feet once, and not long ago. They have raised those railroad embankments up, and shut off the old world that was behind them. Climb up that bank on which the irons are laid, and look to the other side—it is gone.[30]

The trains and canals that changed the landscape were built to connect factories to ports. As industrialists built more and more factories, many small rural villages along transport routes grew into large ugly cities, further obliterating the pastoral landscape. Most noticeable was the smoke that hovered over the cities, adding to England's reputation for fog. Fumes mingled with the fog, fouling the air, especially where chemical plants were located. And all over the island once crystal clear streams and rivers became murky as factories dumped their waste into them. Around cities where industries processed iron into steel, waste called slag "spread, acre by acre, over what had hitherto been green fields."[31] As the era wore on, industrialists cluttered the roads and railway lines with billboards, advertising consumer goods from Beecham's Pills to Lipton Tea.

LIFE FOR ENGLAND'S FARMERS

Just as the coming of industry changed England's green rural landscape, the same force modified England's rural way of life. Changes were introduced that altered centuries-old economic and social patterns. For example, in the late 1700s a series of enclosure acts transferred to the owners of large, private estates thousands of acres that had been open to all. The enclosure of the common fields and pastures that had surrounded villages meant more efficient farming, since land that had served as farm laborers' hunting grounds and small gardens now could be devoted to the owners' cash crops. The change yielded more farmland for the early agribusinessmen, but it ruined the small farmers, known as yeomen. Many of these proud, independent Britons then had to resort to tenant farming for a living. Historian Altick explains the demoralizing effect of this process:

> The decline of the yeomen as a class was among the most regrettable developments that drastically changed the nature of rural society, for it was they who, in [novelist] George Eliot's words in *The Mill on the Floss,* "dressed in good broadcloth, paid high rates and taxes, went to church, and ate a particularly good dinner on Sunday." . . . For centuries the yeomen had represented solidity, prosperity, decency, independence; they had been beholden to no man; in time of natural crisis their courage made them the very personification of the English "hearts of oak."[32]

While yeomen lost their farms and their standard of living declined, the large estate owners for a time continued to prosper. In the 1870s, however, bad weather and cheap imported grain would bring prices down, affecting all farmers.

The former yeomen and the traditional small tenant farmers working one hundred acres of rented land lived simple subsistence lives through most of the Victorian period. On a typical day a farmer would rise early and set the crew of laborers to their tasks; then he might shoot or fish for food and sport, or maintain the property. For entertainment he sang with the men's chorus, played cards, and visited with friends of the same social class. Except for occasional hunts, farmers rarely interacted with the gentry.

The difference in manners and education between the working class and the gentry was too great for socializing at familiar levels. These small farmers were solid citizens, but because they lacked the sophistication that education provides, they seldom partook in running local affairs. They might serve as church wardens, but not local magistrates. They allowed some education for their daughters to give them greater polish and a chance to find rich husbands, but they saw little benefit in book learning for their sons. Even when schools were available, farmers saw such things as books, equipment, and salaries for educated teachers as extravagances unnecessary in their daily lives.

SURVIVAL EXISTENCE FOR FARM LABORERS

The tenant farmers employed unskilled farm laborers to help with the work during busy times of planting and harvest. Farmers gave laborers an allowance, which usually amounted to a rent-free cottage, food at

A farmer pauses to observe an upper-class man hunting. The highly stratified Victorian society prevented much interaction among different social classes.

THE WIDENING GAP BETWEEN RICH AND POOR

With the advent of the enclosure system in rural England and the factory system in the cities, lives of laborers became progressively more dismal. Meanwhile, a new breed of middle class moved upward in society to greater comforts.

In *Victorian England: Portrait of an Age,* G. M. Young suggests that the traditional image of England, "with its bold peasants and happy children" had vanished. In rural England the enclosure system resulted in a society split into owners and workers. There were a few well-managed villages, where responsible landlords and an activist clergy provided income supplements for men with families and schools for children. Most villages were neglected, and their inhabitants, like those living in the large towns, were perishing. After what work men were able to find, they lounged and drank, and their neglected sons and daughters failed to learn the skills necessary to manage a family.

Large cities also grew increasingly more divided into the rich and the poor. Young reports that factory employers "were moving into the country; their officials followed them into the suburbs; [and] the better workmen lived in the better streets." The poor were crowded into slums and cellars, living in makeshift dwellings hastily thrown up by speculative builders or in deserted tenements formerly occupied by the upper classes. Abandoned by the old ruling class and their former leaders, the poor were left to survive, if they could, "unpoliced, ungoverned, and unschooled." Young follows this grim summary with a distressing depiction of life in mid-nineteenth-century Britain:

> But the imagination can hardly apprehend the horror in which thousands of families [back then] were born, dragged out their ghastly lives, and died; the drinking water brown with faecal particles, the corpses kept unburied for a fortnight in a festering London August; mortified limbs quivering with maggots; courts [courtyards] where not a weed would grow, and sleeping-dens afloat with sewage.

And while the new proletariat [working class] was falling below the median line of improving decency on one side, the middle classes were rising above it on the other, becoming progressively more regular, more sober, more clean in body, more delicate in speech.

harvest time, milk, and potatoes, but the cash wages did not cover such essentials as boots and clothing. Some lived in one-room hovels housing both parents and children, as many as thirteen people, in one instance. Some farm laborers' children went to work at eight years of age, scaring birds away from newly planted corn or helping their fathers with odd jobs. One twelve-year-old boy said, "I know that twice ten is twenty, because I have heard other boys say so. I cannot read," and another said, "When I am not at work I do not often get bread and meat for dinner. . . . I had rather work than play."[33] Farm laborers' wives worked in the fields along with the men, sometimes eleven hours a day in haytime. In the fall after harvest, they went gleaning with their daughters. On a good day a mother and three daughters might pick up six bushels of grain from the leavings of the harvesters.

Few opportunities existed for the children of rural laborers to escape this meager, hard existence. Families tried to place girls as servants in homes of good families when they were between ten and fifteen years old. Though a maid's job was hard work, a servant girl was fed, clothed, and housed. Boys might enlist in the army though living accommodations were poor and rations limited until the 1850s, or they might immigrate to one of the colonies, an option that became less dangerous and uncomfortable toward the end of the century. Most who left the village migrated to large cities to work in the factories, hoping to find better lives there. Census figures from 1851 show that 1.2 million men and 143,000 women worked on farms; in 1901 there were 700,000 men and 12,000 women in farm occupations.

WORKING AND LIVING IN FACTORY CITIES

Life in rural England through most of the Victorian era was unrewarding and difficult, but the better life hoped for in the factory cities was, at least during the first half of Queen Victoria's reign, little or no better. The Lancashire cotton mill typified the prominent textile industry; mills in other cities were nearly identical. The mill was a six-story building with forty windows on each floor. It was lighted by gas that heated the room and fouled the air. Altick describes conditions:

> They [the workers] were deafened by the noise of the steam engines and the clattering machinery and stifled in air that not only was laden with dust but, in the absence of ventilation, was heated to as high as eighty-five degrees. The workers were driven to maximum output by strict overseers, fined for spoiling goods, dozing off, looking out the window, and other derelictions, and forever imperiled by unguarded shafts, belts, and flywheels. Industrial diseases and those caused simply by the proximity of many unwashed chronically ill human bodies conspired with accidents to disable and kill them.[34]

Under these conditions men, women, and children labored for as many as fourteen to sixteen hours a day, six days a week.

Shortly before Victoria became queen, working hours for children between nine and thirteen had been limited, but young children were still exploited in some of the mills and in other kinds of factories.

After a long workday in the mill, workers went home to apartment-style buildings provided by mill owners. Many of these complexes, built back to back with a common wall, were as dismal as the cottages provided for rural farmworkers and more crowded. Water was available for an hour a day, at a pipe often located a considerable distance from the housing. Sometimes as many as forty families shared a common outdoor toilet. An underground sewage system had yet to be invented, so waste collected in open-air drains, but no water was available to wash it away. There was no street lighting, and smoke, belching from coal-burning furnaces, filled the air and covered everything with gray soot. In a famous passage from his novel *Hard Times*, Charles Dickens describes Coketown, an imaginary factory town that resembled Lancashire and all other factory towns like it:

Charles Dickens experienced firsthand the brutal factory conditions during the Victorian era. The building at left is the blacking factory where Dickens worked at age twelve.

It was a town of red brick, or of brick that would have been red if the smoke and ashes had allowed it; but as matters stood it was a town of unnatural red and black like the painted face of a savage. It was a town of machinery and tall chimneys, out of which interminable serpents of smoke trailed themselves forever and ever, and never got uncoiled. It had a black canal in it, and a river that ran purple with ill-smelling dye, and vast piles of buildings full of windows where there was a rattling and trembling all day long, and where the piston of the steam-engine worked monotonously up and down like the head of an elephant in a state of melancholy madness. It contained several large streets all very like one another, and many small streets still more like one another, inhabited by people equally like one another, who all went in and out at the same hours, with the same sound upon the same pavements, to do the same work, and to whom every day was the same as yesterday and tomorrow, and every year the counterpart of the last and the next.[35]

Slums like these were breeding grounds for disease, which broke out periodically in epidemics, and despair, which was an understandable response to so much misery.

Not all factory owners, however, exploited their workers. In Yorkshire, for example, mill owner Sir Titus Salt moved his large mill to open country and laid out

Although most factories were dangerous, filthy workplaces, a few provided a healthy, pleasant environment for the laborers.

Legally, working hours for children were restricted, but some business owners ignored the law and worked boys and girls as young as five up to fourteen hours a day.

the town of Saltshire around it. The houses he built had a parlor, a kitchen, two or three bedrooms, and a backyard. Saltshire had a school, a church, and a park along the river. A few other owners followed Salt's example, but most of them thought only of "how many cottages could be built upon the smallest space of ground and at the least possible cost."[36]

EXPLOITED WORKERS IN SMALL FACTORIES AND MINES

Though the cotton mills are cited most frequently as symbols of the factory system, owners of other kinds of factories and businesses also exploited workers. Craftsmen, who paid rates based on the number of pieces produced, were some of the worst exploiters of children. Their businesses and factories were small, and the work load was irregular, sometimes forcing shutdowns for days and sometimes requiring workers, including children, to catch up by working fifteen or sixteen hours a day. The production of handprinted wallpaper and pottery was typically carried out in small factories like these. Small boys between six and ten carried molds from the potters to the stoves in small rooms where the temperature rose to 120 degrees. In match factories, women and children suffered from phosphorus contamination, a condition that damaged the jaws and teeth. Girls as young as five were propped up and tapped on the head to keep them awake to stitch gloves ordered on short notice. These operations, the first sweatshops, sprang up amid the large factories and in the mining towns where there were large congregations of workers.

To run the steam engines that ran the trains and factory machinery, England needed an increasing supply of coal. Consequently, the mining industry grew as rapidly as other industries; the number of coal miners grew from 69,600 in 1801 to more than 200,000 in 1850. Men, women, and children working in the mines endured some of the worst conditions of the industrial revolution. Miners worked deep in the ground in dark shafts, or seams, lighted only by candles, which burned out or tipped over and caused accidents. In 1815, safety lamps were introduced, but they produced less light than candles. Ventilation was bad, coal dust filled the air, and water and rats ran in the seams. Hewers—those who loosened the coal chunks—worked on their knees in seams often as narrow as eighteen inches. Putters, who moved carts full of coal in three-foot-high passages, had to push their loads bent at the waist or drag them on hands and knees.

Though the most physically taxing work in the mines was given to men, mine owners also found jobs for women and children. Women and girls worked as putters, wearing wide leather belts with a chain passing between their legs to attach the truck. Women in Scotland's mines worked as bearers, carrying baskets filled with a hundredweight (112 pounds) of coal through the passages and up ladders to the pit top. Historian Bernard A. Cook describes how the children worked:

Young girls and boys were assigned to negotiate baskets through the narrowest seams. Children from five to eight years old were employed as trappers. Isolated and in pitch dark, their job was to open and shut the doors in the passages which controlled ventilation. Since the trappers were among the first to go down into the pits and the last to come up, these children were underground about fourteen hours a day.[37]

With the huge influx of families to mining areas, mine owners sponsored housing projects just as the factory owners did, and similar towns with the same dismal conditions developed near the mines.

COPING WITH POVERTY IN BIG-CITY SLUMS

Not all cities with rapidly growing populations were factory or mining towns. London grew both from the influx of people from rural areas and from large numbers immigrating from abroad; by 1850 nearly half of the people living in London were born outside of England. Unlike industrial cities, where people sought factory or mining jobs, London attracted people looking for jobs in the trades and professions. As people poured in, the city grew from the small center that is London proper to include the surrounding boroughs, or urban incorporated areas. In 1862 French historian Hippolyte Taine viewed London with awe: "Three million five hundred thousand inhabitants: it adds up to twelve cities the size of Marseilles, ten as big as Lyons, two the size of Paris, in a single mass. . . . Enormous, enormous—that is the word which recurs all the time."[38]

As soon as the railways extended beyond London, those who could afford to move to adjacent suburbs did, leaving the city center inhabited by the poor. Poverty was widespread in London, and no social programs existed at the beginning of Victoria's reign to alleviate the worst conditions. If workers took sick or lost their jobs, no governmental institutions were available to help them. In the absence of an accurate system for taking the census, there are no precise statistics indicating how many people lived in poverty. Studies estimate, however, that a third to half of grown men lived in poverty. Poverty affected women more adversely than it affected men, who escaped the squalor of their homes to spend time and money in the pubs. A nurse who knew the London poor said that many a man gave his wife a small sum and expected that "she ought to be able to, because in many cases she does, feed four children, dress them and herself, and pay rent."[39]

Poverty resulted from unemployment, underemployment, and wages held low by the abundance of workers. Moreover, some

One of the side effects of the industrial revolution was the creation of slums, urban neighborhoods where residents suffered extreme poverty and unsanitary conditions.

workers were laid off when seasonal work was done; others were laid off during the frequent downturns in the economy. Unskilled workers in what was called casual employment lived their entire lives in poverty. Journalist and sociologist Henry Mayhew investigated the casual working class (self-employed, part-time workers) in the 1840s and called it "all that large class who live by either selling, showing, or doing something through the country . . . street-folk—street-sellers, street-buyers, street-finders, street-performers, street-artisans or working pedlars and street-labourers."[40] Historian W. John Smith reports that "thousands lived by scavenging off the streets, waterfront, sewers, and garbage dumps. Everything seems to have a market, even dog dung—purchased by tanners in Bermondsey for purifying leather."[41]

A large number of men never knew steady employment and hoped only to find odd jobs lasting a few days or weeks. One sociologist observed that these men spent many hours on the street; a "noticeable thing in poor streets is the mark left on the exterior of the houses. All along the front, about on a level with the hips, there is a broad dirty mark, showing where the men and lads are in the constant habit of standing, leaning a bit forward, as they smoke their pipes, and watch whatever may be going on in the streets."[42]

Victorian England's city streets were crowded with people trying to scrape together money by selling wares, scavenging, or performing.

COPING WITH OVERCROWDING IN BIG-CITY SLUMS

In cities like London and Bath, overcrowding was a major problem. Some slum housing had been torn down to make way for railways and terminals; warehouses replaced other slum properties, and none was replaced by what is now called new affordable housing. Consequently, the city poor crowded into large houses abandoned by those who could afford to move out of the central city. Historians Hilary and Mary Evans explain that because of the influx of impoverished renters, landlords did not have to make these makeshift apartments livable:

> There was every encouragement towards overcrowding, none towards improving the premises or doing anything except ensure that they did not actually fall down and thus lose their value as a source of income. One room in the building . . . houses seven people—one bed sleeping a man, three teenage daughters and their brother, the other their lodgers, a man and his wife. In another room, four families—eighteen persons in all—lived with one bed per family, with no partitions or privacy of any sort.[43]

Sanitation in such crowded conditions was appalling. Indoor toilets, when they existed, could remain broken for months. As in the factory cities, as many as forty families shared a common outdoor toilet. According to Reader, "To the household refuse and human filth there was often added the filth of animals, for many families, following in less suitable surroundings the old cottagers' tradition, kept pigs or fowls in the backyard."[44]

Water supplies were no better than sanitation conditions. People had to carry water from tanks or get it from a water pipe a distance away. A man in Bath had to walk a quarter mile for a bucket of water to use for drinking and tea. For cooking and dishwashing, people used muddy, smelly river water. A Lancashire man said "he never washed his body; he let his shirt rub the dirt off, though he added, 'I wash my neck and ears and face, of course.'"[45]

Cooking and washing dishes with sewage-contaminated water is a surefire way to spread diseases transmitted by contact with infected fecal material. One such disease is cholera, which causes violent diarrhea, vomiting, and rapid dehydration of the body. This dreaded illness reached epidemic proportions in London in 1831–1832. Ten years later, barrister and journalist Edwin Chadwick published *Report on the Sanitary conditions of the Labouring population,* a document that shocked the nation. Altick describes the public reaction: "Never before had so much earnest public discussion . . . been devoted to subjects like cesspools, sewers, and the quality of the water supply."[46] Chadwick proposed some valid public health measures, although he backed them with incorrect reasoning. For example, he proposed ridding the city of open sewers and exposed rotting corpses because he thought that disease was caused by bad odors. Chadwick's ideas were rejected as too expensive, however, and

CONTROVERSY OVER CAUSES OF CHOLERA

Howard C. Baker's essay "Cholera," published in Victorian Britain: An Encyclopedia, *edited by Sally Mitchell, recounts the various theories proposed to explain the causes of the three cholera epidemics that occurred in England between 1831 and 1866.*

"Prior to the discovery of *Vibrio cholerae* in 1883 and acceptance of the germ theory of cholera in the 1890s, British doctors differed over the nature of the disease and the manner of its transmission. During the first epidemic, doctors tended either a 'contagionist' explanation that cholera was transmitted from person to person, or a 'miasmatist' explanation that the disease was produced by noxious exhalations arising from sewage and the like. By midcentury, the promotion of miasmatism by Edwin Chadwick (1800–1890) and other public health reformers made it the dominant theory. In 1849 and 1854 [scientist] John Snow (1813–1858) in London attempted to demonstrate that cholera was a 'poison' transmitted by water. Scientifically plausible refutations of Snow's theory put forth by miasmatists meant that it was accepted only by a minority of doctors by 1866.

In 1831–32 the Privy Council created a temporary arrangement of local boards of health guided by a Central Board of Health in London for the prevention and treatment of cholera. These authorities encountered opposition from political radicals who suspected that 'cholera' was a sham perpetrated by the government to serve the interests of the medical profession and sometimes violent resistance from the poor, who often believed that cholera was introduced into their neighborhoods to provide victims for dissection by the anatomists [medical researchers who attempted to learn about the human body from autopsy investigations, a practice many opposed]. During the later epidemics local management of cholera was left to the regular local authorities and, in 1853–1854 and in 1866, to the new permanent boards of health established by a number of communities. The heightened social tension characteristic of the first epidemic was largely absent in later outbreaks."

with failure to eliminate the unsanitary conditions, there were three more epidemics, killing 140,000.

A BETTER LIFE FOR SOME SKILLED WORKERS

Some members of the working class fared better than the unskilled poor and lived more comfortably, though not as well as middle-class entrepreneurs. Skilled workers, eager to separate themselves from the poorest slum dwellers, had better opportunities for regular employment and higher incomes. The skilled workers included retail tradespeople and clerks in shops. Other skilled workers were employed in the building industry, such as masons and carpenters; others worked in the metal industry, forging products in iron and steel. Those in publishing were skilled at typesetting, and many more were "scattered in key positions and often in small numbers throughout manufacturing industry, mining and transport."[47] The new industrial society also created many new occupations in, for example, the railway service and the food industry. Workers who were flexible and able to learn new skills obtained positions and enjoyed secure employment. These skilled workers enjoyed better housing, better food, and better clothing than the unskilled poor in central London.

THE DEVELOPMENT OF SUBURBS

As central London became crowded with immigrants and the rising local population, the upper middle class moved to the edge of the city and to nearby villages, forming a ring of suburbs. Before the suburban railways, commuters traveled by horse-drawn buses, and few chose to live more than about six miles from London. When the railways established daily operations, suburbs sprang up as far as thirty miles from the city. Historian Harry Schalck explains the social attitudes toward suburban living:

> The suburban movement represented a major change in the way Victorians and their descendants lived. Separate from but always linked socially and economically to cities, the suburbs featured homes separated from workplaces and major cultural institutions, an emphasis on family life in a healthful, even bucolic [rural] setting, and freedom from urban overcrowding and industrial defilement with their resulting social ills, including crime. "Suburbia" was a state of mind developed in the early nineteenth century by the upper middle class.[48]

In the early Victorian years, when suburban living became a symbol of wealth, the middle class built elaborate and ostentatious homes designed to impress friends and business associates. By 1880 writers and journalists, calling suburbs "villadom," mocked these new communities as dull places inhabited by dull people.

Historians consider the development of suburbs to be one of the spinoff effects of the industrial revolution. The more profound effects, such as the death of the agrarian society and the birth of a new manufacturing technology, combined with the growth in population, had immense impact on the whole of England. Change occurred rapidly, and Britain had neither adequate laws nor appropriate institutions to deflect the turmoil and suffering that came with the changes, especially to the working poor. In the 1830s, the decade in which Victoria became queen, the public was beginning to protest publicly against poverty, and writers and intellectuals had begun debating major social issues.

Chapter

4 Poverty, Protests, and Politicians

The upheavals caused by population growth and industrialism produced large numbers of poor people in both rural areas and cities, and the early Victorian politicians did little to help them. As conditions deteriorated for the working poor, they began agitating for change. When the upper and middle classes failed to respond to their needs, tensions mounted and the threat of class warfare was in the air. Desperate poor workers believed they needed and deserved help, since they had neither economic nor political power. The middle classes, however, blamed the poor people themselves for being poor and discouraged welfare measures, believing that individual effort and hard work could solve all problems. Upper-class politicians feared anarchy and revolution. The bloody French Revolution of 1789 was a vivid memory, and British aristocrats were anxious to avoid a similar outcome in England.

1834 POOR LAWS REFLECT UPPER- AND MIDDLE-CLASS ATTITUDES

Historically the Poor Laws had aided those in poverty. Between 1531 and 1601,

Poor Laws were enacted first to allow begging and then to encourage voluntary almsgiving to orphans, the sick, the elderly, and those unable to find work. Legislation passed between 1598 and 1601 levied funds to make regular government payments to the poor and to create jobs for those able to work. This arrangement, dating from the early seventeenth century, prevailed until the dislocation of people caused by the enclosure system and industrialism swelled the ranks of unemployed workers facing poverty, and taxpayers objected to the rising costs.

In 1834 the prevailing Poor Law was revised, introducing the workhouse. Cities built no-frills facilities called workhouses, where unemployed men and their families could live. Sponsors of the revision urged that able-bodied men receive relief only in a local workhouse and that they not be paid enough to achieve the standard of living affordable by the lowest-paid job holder. For shelter and bread, workers spent their days breaking stones or grinding corn. Historian Mark Neuman explains other provisions:

> Inmates of the workhouse were to be housed in separate areas according to age and sex, married couples were

Unemployed men could stay at workhouses, government-funded facilities where they worked in exchange for room and board.

separated, and until 1842 parents had no right to see their children. Between the ages of five and fourteen orphans and the children of paupers were to be lodged in separate Poor Law schools and could be hired out or apprenticed by the overseers. A further provision made mothers solely responsible for illegitimate children.[49]

The rules were intended to discourage laziness, to encourage those who had jobs to save money in preparation for times of unemployment or illness, and to discourage unmarried women from becoming pregnant. As another modern historian,

David Newsome, writes, however, the poor themselves attributed the following attitude to the authors of the new Poor Law:

> Take it or leave it. If you won't work, or if you choose to be a pauper (which is not the same thing as being poor), you can come inside the workhouse, and we shall do our best to make your life that much less congenial than anything you can find for yourself outside. We won't have people coming here to shirk work.[50]

The middle-class moral attitudes and actions outraged the poor and raised tensions between the classes. The poor, having seen assistance given more generously in the past, felt they were being unfairly treated since, after all, the economic problems were not their fault. Moreover, the workhouse system humiliated them. The middle class, on the other hand, believed their behavior modification program of forced labor would curb laziness, and the unattractive workhouse setting would encourage poor men to choose hard work instead. With these attitudes, it was morally acceptable to say that ignoring the poor or treating them harshly was for their own good.

Some people in the middle class held religious attitudes that interpreted Scripture in ways that justified their inclination to ignore the plight of the poor. For example, they believed that since God rewards virtue and punishes vice, the poor were being punished; if they practiced sobriety, worked hard, and were devoted to their masters' wishes, they would be rewarded by not being poor. Moreover, Reader says, "the good Bible-reading Christian was inclined to take a rather fatalistic view of the whole affair. Had it not been said, on the highest authority [the Bible], 'the poor ye have always with you'?"[51] Esmé Wingfield-Stratford writes that

> one minister of Christ would even abolish the poor law, and leave the helpless veteran and superfluous infant to find charity or die in the nearest ditch. He is a little perturbed, though, at the thought of charity. Un-

less "the hand of benevolence" is restrained [according to this extreme Victorian], idleness and improvidence will thrive.[52]

An additional reason for not helping the poor was economic. Many from the middle class had become the owners of factories and mines and viewed the hordes of poor workers as a convenient pool of cheap labor for their industries. These industrialists preferred to keep the unemployed poor out of workhouses so that they would be available for hire in response to sudden requirements for more manpower. Thus, the unemployed poor workers were caught between low wages and the workhouse.

POPULAR THEORIES ENCOURAGE NEGLECT OF THE POOR

Middle-class Victorians further justified their attitudes toward the poor on the basis of prevalent theories espoused by contemporary philosophers and economists. According to one theory, exploiting cheap labor was "natural." The argument went like this: Humans naturally strive for what pleases them most and try to achieve those things with the least amount of self-denial and pain. Striving for material success was natural and good, but spending hard-earned money to help the poor was painful; thus it was natural and good to avoid the pain and self-denial that would result from providing such assistance. Those who held these views tended to justify the exploitation of cheap labor as "natural," hence not morally wrong.

Another popular theory was laissez-faire. This French term literally means letting people do as they please, but in an economic sense it describes opposition to government interference in the conduct of business. Thus proponents of laissez-faire believed "that somehow 'nature' had arranged that the prosperity of the individual—he who won out in the eternal competition of the marketplace—would automatically result in the public good."[53] Because pursuing profits resulted in the "public good," by encouraging investment and creating new jobs, competing

Most middle-class Victorians believed that poverty was a result of laziness.

industrialists were not wrong to take advantage of the large workforce by paying as little as possible. Moreover, the government should not restrict such competition by regulating industry or stepping in on behalf of the poor.

Yet another prevailing theory contributing to the middle-class attitude toward poor workers was reflected in the rules of the 1834 Poor Law. This theory, proposed by economist and sociologist Thomas Malthus, held that the population grew faster than the food supply could increase. As a result, unless the number of children born was restricted, an overcrowded world would fall victim to periodic disasters in which many died, lowering the population and supposedly restoring the balance. On the basis of this belief, men and women were separated in the workhouse to reduce the birthrate among the poor and protect the balance between population and food supply. Furthermore, helping the poor, the Malthusians felt, would almost certainly encourage them to keep having children, in turn endangering the food supply.

EXPLOITATION AND NEGLECT SPUR THE POOR TO RIOT

Exposure to all these attitudes and theories contributed to upper- and middle-class Victorians' inclination to ignore the conditions of the poor. Yet despite exploitation and neglect, their numbers continued to grow as children were born in the slums and poor foreigners continued to immigrate. Periodically, their patience

RIOTS CREATE FEAR OF REVOLUTION AMONG LEADERS

Unemployment, low wages, and hunger led desperate working-class men in rural areas and cities to gather in large crowds to call attention to their distress. When conditions were at their worst and political leaders seemed to turn a deaf ear, riots broke out. The Peterloo Massacre in Manchester symbolizes the fears and frustrations of the class conflict that eventually led to reforms beginning in the 1830s. In The Victorian Age 1815–1914, *R. J. Evans explains how the ferment escalated.*

"Accompanying the search for food were wild excesses of violence in which villagers, led by a fictitious 'Captain Swing', avenged themselves on the local landlord by burning his ricks [haystacks] and farm buildings, or turning loose his valuable stock to wander where they liked. . . .

But the distress was much greater among the mass of working people in the towns, especially in the north. Unemployment was chronic and widespread. . . . The year 1816 was particularly bad, because in addition to an Irish potato shortage, the English harvest was also a failure.

In the winter bread riots took place in the big towns of the Midlands and the North, accompanied by the machine-smashing riots of the Luddites [workers who rioted and destroyed labor-saving textile machinery in the belief that such machinery would diminish employment]. London itself did not escape. . . .

Another bad harvest and a drop in trade produced in 1819 a repetition of the events of 1816–17, . . . and the Government was exposed to the full blast of a growing demand for parliamentary reforms as the only cure for the nation's evils. Disorder broke out in all the leading towns, and culminated at Manchester on August 16th when 'Orator' Hunt [a farmer's son] addressed a crowd of fifty thousand people. The magistrates lost their heads, attempted to arrest Hunt, and finally ordered the Yeomanry [conservative small farmers who had not joined the protest] to disperse the crowd: a piece of panic-stricken folly which resulted in several deaths and hundreds of injuries. The Manchester Massacre, or Battle of Peterloo, showed like a flash of lightning the gulf which separated the English people from their Government."

and passivity turning to anger, the poor took steps to organize and act in order to call attention to their plight. Consequently, riots occurred in many parts of England for more than a decade. At first, unemployed skilled workers rioted to protest the loss of their livelihood as machines in factories eliminated their jobs in small shops. In addition, poor workers periodically rioted over the high price of bread. The tariffs that kept grain prices high were permanently abolished in 1848, but until that time the Tory government, frightened that chaos might prevail, took firm measures to control mob demonstrations, a stance that further angered the poor workers.

A series of protests occurred in the early 1830s, when workers were joined by protestors from the middle class who wanted the right to vote. Mob leaders believed that political leaders had to be intimidated into choosing between a reform bill and a revolution. Recurring riots erupted between November 1830 and March 1831; during that period 1,400 rioters were taken to court, 9 were sentenced to hang, 652 were imprisoned, and 464 were deported to colonies. The worst riot occurred in the fall of 1831 in Bristol, where rioters burned the Bishop's Palace, looted houses and shops, and released prisoners from jail. Historian and writer Charles Kingsley had been present at the riot and later offered his version of it:

> The brave, patient soldiers sitting . . . motionless on their horses, the blood streaming from wounds on their heads and faces, waiting for the order which the miserable, terrified Mayor had not courage to give; the savage, brutal, hideous mob of inhuman wretches plundering, destroying, burning; casks of spirit broken open and set flaming in the streets, the wretched creatures drinking it on their knees from the gutter, till the flame from a burning house caught the stream, ran down it with a horrible rushing sound, and, in one dreadful moment, the prostrate drunkards had become a row of blackened corpses.[54]

THE FIRST MINIMAL REFORM

The Whig government of Lord Charles Grey, committed to reform, replaced the Tory government in 1830 and went to work to draft the Reform Act, which passed in 1832. This legislation increased the percentage of voters from 11 to 18 percent of the male population by granting voting rights to all propertied adult males. For the first time, about half of the men in the middle classes could vote, but none from the working classes. This act also changed boundaries of southern rural boroughs to make representation in Parliament more proportional, but it left the densely populated cities in the north without representation. Finally, it initiated a form of registration to prevent dishonest politicians from paying voters to cast multiple ballots. The working classes were sorely disappointed, as was most of the middle class, when the promised reform gave them no political power and no help.

The period from 1837 to 1849 was particularly volatile and tensions could have exploded at any time. Severe economic depression had closed many factories and laid off workers; machines had replaced tens of thousands of workers, adding to unemployment; harvests were bad and food was scarce; and the cholera epidemic of 1848–1849 killed over sixty thousand. Moreover, the Factory Act of 1833, which reduced working hours for children, did nothing to improve the lot of adults. The 1834 Poor Law, with its offensive implications that the poor were simply lazy, was particularly resented.

Millions of people who thought the political establishment was indifferent were angry enough to be easily aroused when

Lord Charles Grey, England's prime minister from 1830 to 1834.

Irish newspaperman Fergus O'Connor threatened the use of force in his paper the *North Star*. His article gave rise to the slogan, "Peacefully if we may, forcibly if we must."[55] That slogan, in turn, provided the seeds of Chartism, the first working-class movement in modern English history.

CHARTISM URGES REAL REFORM

The Chartists were a loose federation of disillusioned workingpeople from all parts of England with a variety of grievances. The name comes from the People's Charter, a bill of rights delivered to Parliament in the form of a petition in 1839 following riots. When Parliament passed but then ignored it, Chartists presented it again in 1842 and 1848. Again Parliament ignored it both times. The People's Charter made six demands: universal suffrage, secret voting, no property qualifications for MPs (members of Parliament), salary for MPs so that poor people could seek election, annual elections to Parliament, and electoral districts with proportionately equal representation.

The Chartists caused enough uproar in 1848 to frighten the establishment. Fergus O'Connor, now an MP, summoned Chartists and threatened to march on London, stage a huge demonstration, and present Parliament with a monstrous petition with 5 million names. In command of the defense of London was the Duke of Wellington. The aging military hero, who had defeated Napoléon at the Battle of Waterloo, surrounded the major points of attack, and

WORKERS MEET TO PROTEST BREAD PRICES AND POVERTY

On February 15, 1846, the newspaper London Observer *covered a protest rally where peasants explained that their poverty was caused by tariffs on grain known as the Corn Laws, and the "bread-taxing oligarchy." The article appears in* The Observer of the Nineteenth Century. (*The wages cited are expressed in shillings (s). At the time, a shilling was worth about 24 cents.*)

"It was a meeting of the local peasantry, held to interchange the sad history of their slow starvation. It had originated entirely with the working men. . . . The proceedings commenced soon after seven, when there were probably about 1,500 persons present—clustered in a dense mass round the stone cross of the market place, and the canvas tent. A labourer, Job Gingel, took the chair. . . .

'My friends—I be a labouring man, I have a wife and seven children in my family. My wages at the present time is 8s. a week (cries of 'you can't live on that—you cant'). In the beginning of December last I only got 7s. . . . I do ask what the Wiltshire labourer has done, or what crimes he has committed, that he be so deprived of necessaries—that he be worse off than the convicts on board the hulks (loud cheers)? . . . Oh, friends . . . the hunger and distress which we have been lying under so long be owing to the Corn-laws (cheers). . . .'

John Batchelor, of Pewsey, a labourer, was the next speaker. For the last fortnight he had only received 6s. a week. He knew many men with four children who had only 6s. and 5s. (shame). For himself he did not know what to do. He expected to be discharged when he got home for having come to the meeting. . . . 'It be them Corn-laws, them cursed Corn-laws, which made bread dear,' [he said]."

O'Connor called off the march on Parliament. Predictably enough, Parliament ignored the People's Charter again. After 1848 the Chartist movement died from lack of organization and leadership. It nonetheless had a profound long-term effect: Within the next century all of the Chartists' demands were enacted into law, except one—annual elections to Parliament.

Historians, who take a long perspective, have observed that both sides—the workers and the establishment—won. The workers eventually received the gains they had sought, and the establishment averted revolution throughout the Victorian period. Newsome explains:

On the whole, right through Victoria's reign, successive governments were wily enough never to allow class conflict to harden to the point where wide-scale violence was inevitable. Concessions might come late, but some measure of conciliation was usually offered before the dam burst. . . . But what a historian can discern by looking backwards is not necessarily what contemporaries are able to appreciate by looking inwards. [Philosopher] Bertrand Russell knew enough of his grandfather Lord John Russell's anxieties to write: "It is not always easy to realise in reading history that the actors in any period, unlike ourselves, did not know the future. We know that Victorian England developed peaceably, but the contemporaries of the Chartists did not know this."[56]

WRITERS CRITICIZE SOCIETY AND CALL FOR REFORM

The fear of violent revolution was indeed a factor that influenced Parliament to initiate reforms, but MPs were also influenced by intellectuals and writers whose steady commentary on the upheavals of the time contributed to the formation of public opinion. On one hand, writers protested the machinelike mentality that disregarded human needs in favor of a seemingly obsessive drive for wealth and material goods. On the other hand, they exposed the conditions of poor workers and urged reforms that would improve their plight. Between 1830 and 1850 the public acclaimed these writers, and their

works were widely read in popular magazines. According to Hazelton Spencer, the writers saw themselves as "a modern priesthood whose duty was to enlighten and encourage and purify public opinion."[57] Numerous essayists, a few poets, and many novelists turned to virtual full-time criticism of their society.

Two literary men, Matthew Arnold and Thomas Carlyle, delivered particularly sharp attacks. Arnold, better known to modern readers for his poems, such as "Dover Beach," than for his social criticism, attacked middle-class materialism, saying that "people needed a higher conception of progress and a sounder basis for national pride than bigger and faster machines and greater and greater wealth."[58] Essayist Thomas Carlyle was critical of both materialism and the neglect of the poor. He fired an attack on what he called "the Condition-of-England Question," by which he meant the side-by-side existence of great wealth and utter poverty. He called for action to relieve the suffering of the masses: limiting the hours in factories and mines, making the conditions of work safer and more sanitary, public works programs to solve overpopulation and unemployment, and a national system of public schools. In *Past and Present*, Carlyle urged better living conditions in factory towns:

Every toiling Manchester, its smoke and soot all burnt, ought it not, among so many world-wide conquests, to have a hundred acres or so of free green-field, with trees on it, conquered, for its little children to disport in; for its all-conquering workers to

THE REFORM RIOTS

"In the autumn of 1830, the issue of reform was laid squarely before the Duke of Wellington, still the prime minister. He declared that the present system was perfectly adequate. It was a most inopportune moment for him to do so, because fearsome memories of the marauding Luddites of twenty years earlier were stirred by the violence sweeping a dozen counties in the form of agricultural workers' uprising led by a mystical 'Captain Swing.' Haystacks were burned by the hundreds, farmers' houses sacked, their implements broken up, and the countryside terrified. Although the cause of the disturbances was the workers' demand for a decent wage, it was inseparable from the reform fever, and political considerations obviously affected the rioters' punishment. . . .

Now new troubles broke out across the nation. There were riots in London, Birmingham, and elsewhere, and mobs burned the central section of Bristol as well as Nottingham Castle, property of the [unpopular] Duke of Newcastle. . . . To add to the tension, the dreaded cholera was appearing in the ports.

By May, 1832, the great coalition of pro-reform factions was organizing runs on banks; factories were shutting down while employers and employees alike attended mass meetings; the newly reactivated radical press spread news of every instance of protest; the nation's troops were alerted. Throughout the country there was acute fear that a spark would ignite the whole explosive mixture and tear Britain apart."

take a breath of twilight air in? You would say so! A willing Legislature could say so with effect. A willing Legislature could say very many things![59]

This kind of criticism of society's values and activities, repeated often in widely read magazines, helped to modify public opinion and, in turn, influence lawmakers.

Some Victorian poets wove the themes of protest into their works. Poet Elizabeth Barrett Browning took up the cause of working children in a thirteen-stanza poem in which she repeated the theme of children weeping. One stanza aims directly at children working in mines and factories.

"For Oh," say the children, "we are weary,
And we cannot run or leap;
If we cared for any meadows, it were merely
To drop down in them and sleep.
Our knees tremble sorely in the stooping,
We fall upon our faces, trying to go;
And, underneath our heavy eyelids drooping,
The reddest flower would look as pale as snow.
For, all day, we drag our burden tiring,
Through the coal-dark, underground;
Or, all day, we drive the wheels of iron
In the factories, round and round."[60]

The language of poetry was especially powerful in evoking the sympathies of the reading public, who either already sympathized with the poor or were the targets of the poet's propaganda.

The literary genre most often used to expose abuses and to promote legislative reform, however, was the social problem novel. Such books featured fictitious narratives to depict typical industrial situations during the Victorian era. They addressed such issues as conditions and hours of the work, abuse of workers by overseers or middlemen, workers' home lives, and the relationships between middle-class factory owners and their lower-class "hands." Though there were numerous social-problem novelists, Charles Dickens, who blended sympathy and humor, was the most prominent and the most popular. He focused on a particular problem in each of his novels by using settings and characters to expose evil. For example, in *Oliver Twist* he attacked the workhouse system, in *The Old Curiosity Shop*, child labor, in *Nicholas Nickleby*, the flogging and bad food in boarding schools, and in *Hard Times*, his detailed description conveys the soul-destroying work environment in a textile mill.

The greatest value of social protest literature lay in its capacity to arouse public

Essayist and social critic Thomas Carlyle called for widespread reform.

attention and provide information that likely would have been ignored had it been presented to the public in the form of dry sociological data. Reform essays, poems, and novels were written for mass consumption. Joseph Kestner points out that appealing to a wide audience was a way in which "disenfranchised citizens (women, and many men) could bring indirect pressure to bear on lawmakers."[61]

THE TRADE UNIONS

Writers' words were intended to persuade political leaders to make reforms, and riots and violence were threats aimed at upping the ante. There was yet a third way that workers tried to improve their wages and working conditions, and that was through trade unions. In 1800 trade union activity was made illegal, but that law was repealed in 1825. The first trade unions involved skilled workers in a single occupation, such as civil engineers or shoemakers, who united to seek cooperation from managers to secure better pay. After the disappointing Reform Act of 1832, workers' discouragement and anger fueled the trade union movement. Organizers tried to unite the individual skill unions into one overall organization to attain greater influence, but the

A scene from a film production of Oliver Twist, a story by Charles Dickens that shed light on the abuses of the workhouse system.

effort was only partially successful. Since workers were unable to pay dues, the unions lacked money to support workers in case of strikes. One of the largest trade union organizations was the Miners Association of Great Britain, with a hundred thousand members. In 1842 under strong leadership, this union was able to achieve higher living standards and improved mine safety. Not until 1871, when unions were granted legal status, did the unions have the clout to influence management in any consistent way. Despite limitations, historian Steven N. Craig sees positive effects of the trade unions:

> Throughout most of the [nineteenth] century union activity had less effect than one might imagine on the living standards of workers and on the labor market in general. Even when membership was high, worker participation was uneven. Eventually, though, better work conditions, fewer instances of "collective bargaining by riot," more political clout, and a developing working-class consciousness were the fruits of union growth. In 1800 the middle class, the government, and most workers viewed unionism with considerable suspicion. A century later the movement was a viable social, economic, and political force.[62]

UPPER-CLASS POWER AND MIDDLE-CLASS PRESSURE GROUPS

In much of the Victorian era, all power to institute the reforms called for by rioters, writers, and trade unionists was in the hands of upper-class, landowning politicians. Most of the men who gained office in the 1830s, however, were liberal minded and wanted reform. The Whig Party called for moderate reforms that would allow the preservation of the status quo. As historian Angus Hawkins explains, the Whigs supported reforms that would "preserve the respect, gratitude and loyalty of the lower social ranks for the propertied and aristocracy."[63] The Whig government formed by Lord Grey in 1830 was committed to governmental reforms for the purpose of strengthening the power of Parliament and the prime minister. The 1834 government formed by the Tory politician Robert Peel united Parliament and actually initiated social reforms. Peel issued a manifesto proclaiming "his support for moderate reforms 'undertaken in a friendly temper, combining, with firm maintenance of established rights, the correction of proven abuses and the redress of real grievances.'"[64] Thus, Parliament had begun taking small reform measures just before Victoria became queen.

Although the middle class held no seats in Parliament in the first half of the nineteenth century, its members achieved political power by joining pressure groups to influence upper-class MPs. Middle-class Victorians were great joiners of societies, leagues, and orders, some for self-help and others for public service. Pressure groups focused on a single issue to promote reform and influence public policy; historian Eugene L. Rasor identifies many of their creative tactics:

VICTORIAN WRITERS CRITICIZE VICTORIANS

Major Victorian writers criticized the middle class for its preoccupation with money and its neglect of spiritual values. In The Age of Improvement, *Asa Briggs cites the opinion of essayist Thomas Carlyle and analyzes novelist Charles Dickens's view of Victorian hypocrisy.*

"Most of the critics were concerned with the role of money in the new society and the narrowness of outlook of the moneymakers. In the 1840s Carlyle had condemned the 'cash nexus' [the central place of money] and had challenged 'mammon worship' [worship of material wealth]: in the 1860s when the web of credit had stretched further and tighter, Dickens in [the novel] *Our Mutual Friend* (1864–5) drew powerful sketches of the shams and inherent emptiness of the world of mid-Victorian finance. He had always been fascinated by the effect of money on character, and in a brilliant chapter on 'Podsnappery' (Book I, ch. II) looked behind the well-regulated and pre-eminently respectable routine of Mr. Podsnap's life to the shabby 'values' which sustained it. All the elements in Victorianism were sharply criticized in a few pages. Mr. Podsnap lacked taste. 'Hideous solidity was the characteristic of the Podsnap plate [metal eating utensils]. Everything was made to look as heavy as it could, and to take up as much room as possible.' Mr. Podsnap had supreme confidence in his own moral integrity. 'He always knew exactly what Providence meant. Inferior and less respectable men might fall short of that mark, but Mr. Podsnap was always up to it.' Mr. Podsnap sheltered himself from those things in the world which he did not like. 'I don't want to know about it; I don't choose to discuss it; I don't admit it.' Mr. Podsnap believed in sheltering other respectable people too; he felt that there were certain subjects which ought not to be introduced 'among our wives and young persons.' The picture both of high finance and of spiritual poverty in *Our Mutual Friend* had a powerful influence on many discontented mid-Victorians."

They developed and used new tools such as statistics, fact gathering, fund raising, political organizing, and propaganda. Their activities included manipulating voting processes, publishing journals and tracts, accumulating petitions and resolutions, sponsoring speakers and lecturers, hiring agents and agitators, conducting demonstrations and mass meetings, signing and enforcing pledges, and, of course, lobbying members of Parliament and candidates.[65]

Many of the writers and intellectuals were from the middle class and active in pressure groups when these groups were most effective during the first decades of Victoria's reign, from the 1830s to the 1850s.

By the time Victoria came to the throne, a change in attitude—from the notion that the lower "ranks" existed for the convenience of the upper classes to the notion that middle and working classes were entitled to rights of their own—was apparent. While there was indeed an element of goodwill and a sense of justice among MPs, the legislators also acted because they wanted to maintain order and avoid violence and revolution. During this early Victorian period, while workers focused on surviving poverty and improving their conditions and MPs focused on initiating reform and maintaining control of society, the majority of men in the middle classes were preoccupied with making money and improving their own status.

5 The Rise of the Middle Class

By 1850 England had a rich and powerful middle class. Upward mobility had always been a goal and theoretically possible, but before the industrial revolution, the social and economic system had been so tightly structured that moving up in class had been all but impossible. The industrial revolution opened up the system and gave those in the middle class, as well as highly skilled members of the working class, an opportunity to acquire wealth, education, and the social manners of respectability. The highest goal of a striving middle-class man was to be a gentleman of the upper class, defined in the eighteenth century as a wealthy landowner who prided himself in never having to work. In practice, however, members of the middle class often had to settle for small changes in status. Altick comments on the chances for a man to achieve a higher class than the one into which he was born:

> Theoretically there was nothing to prevent a man fired by praiseworthy ambition from rising as high as his talents and exercise of the appropriate prudential virtues [behaving with proper morality and manners] allowed. In

practice, the odds were against it, but now they were not as long as they had been. The possibility, as the spectacular careers of any number of self-made Victorians testified, was there. And unquestionably the general social movement was upward, even if most gains were modest.[66]

Men striving upward needed the discipline of hard work and focus.

A STRATEGY FOR MOVING UPWARD

For years the middle class had seen the best things in life—wealth, property, and social position—awarded to those who acquired them by birth. Now they were determined that men who had ability and drive should be able to seize those privileges. Competent men rose in the middle class by steps. Reader identifies how men "got on," as the middle class called the social climb:

> Socially, that meant moving from manual occupations into 'trade'; from 'trade' into 'the professions'; from 'the professions', ultimately, into 'Society',

where a gentleman's income was assumed to come from his estate. The middle classes might dislike the upper-class way of doing things as long as they felt themselves hindered by it, but that did not for one moment dim their ambition to join the upper class themselves if they could.[67]

Those who did not take the route of trade or the professions sought wealth in business and industry.

Moving upward involved money, work, and competition. Progress meant building capital and then using it to acquire more money (early Victorians seldom considered money something to be spent on personal gratification). To build a supply of money, the middle class developed a special outlook toward work. Thomas Carlyle never tired of proclaiming the sanctity of work regardless of the kind; he said "All work, even cotton spinning, is noble; work is alone noble."[68] The cult of work trained the middle class in discipline and concentration, and striving for money made them fiercely competitive. Historian Esmé Wingfield-Stratford says, "It was not love that moved the sun and the other stars, but merciless competition, . . . with the devil perpetually taking the hindmost and the

The leisurely life of upper-class gentlemen appealed to middle-class workers, who strove to accumulate the money, property, and prestige necessary to climb the social ladder.

fittest surviving."[69] Because the economy went through great booms and great downturns, entrepreneurs and industrialists coped with the risky business environment by requiring hard work of their managers and workers. Those determined to rise could ill afford to indulge themselves or show compassion for others. Wingfield-Stratford says:

> It was by no means unknown for a master to stand in a relation almost paternal to those who toiled for him, but most of them were new men, without traditions, and themselves driven on, by stress of competition, to extract every penny, by almost any means. Humanity was among the many luxuries that these stern and laborious men had to deny themselves.[70]

MIDDLE-CLASS JOBS VARIED

In this age of competition, productivity, and uneven prosperity, middle class Victorians worked in a wide range of jobs. Two factors especially propelled them to success: opportunity and attitude. Historian Elizabeth Burton notes that middle-class entrepreneurs took advantage of expensive new machinery, plants, and mills; a vibrant market; and "a labor force of underpaid men, women and children."[71] They built hundreds of businesses: large shipbuilding companies, iron and steel companies, and breweries; companies making useful products like the soapworks in Bristol; and small craft shops run by skilled artisans. Supporting these new businesses and industries were bankers, traders, and insurance providers. Hundreds of commercial clerks worked for banks, railroads, and manufacturing concerns. The number of merchants and shopkeepers increased because industry produced new products to sell. Newly added to the middle class, but still on the lowest rung of the social ladder, were the highly skilled artisans, such as wallpaper makers, whose services were demanded by the expanding housing market. The social status of workers in any job, however, depended on the amount of money they accumulated.

Middle-class jobs also proliferated in the public sector. The growing population required more government, especially as lawmakers realized that only government reform could improve awful urban conditions. This work required many new civil servants to manage and administer programs. Moreover, the empire was also growing, and England needed administrators, businessmen, and military officers to send to the colonies. Many returned after a tour in the colonies with wealth and middle-class social standing.

In addition, the professions grew both in numbers and in status. Civil engineers were needed to build railways and mechanical engineers to design machinery for factories, lawyers offered professional advice to businessmen, and accountants managed finances for growing enterprises. The growing population needed more doctors and druggists and teachers. Professional men improved their status with education and licensing. During the second half of the century,

Victorian London bustles with activity. The economic boom of the Victorian era introduced many new middle-class jobs, including civil servants, lawyers, and shopkeepers.

when a professional organization required education in addition to apprenticeship and examinations were introduced as a condition of licensing, professionals gained respect and charged higher fees.

By 1850, the middle class had become the dominant class. Workers in a myriad of occupations enjoyed varying degrees of wealth and success. Common to all of them was the competitive drive to climb the social ladder and in the process emulate the style of the classes above them in whatever ways they could.

MIDDLE-CLASS WEALTH REFLECTED IN THE HOME

Middle-class Victorians displayed their wealth and status in their homes. Most of them lived in suburbs of large cities or the outer rings of smaller towns. When convenient transportation made a man's commute to his work in the city a reality, the middle class built detached houses surrounded by as much land as the owner could afford. Having space emulated the upper class, and having a detached house distanced one from workers living in rows of houses with common walls. The middle class built houses with decorative designs and identified their streets with names that suggested elegance—"lanes," "avenues," or "ways." In *The Condition of England,* historian C. F. G. Masterman describes a typical suburb in which the men leave for the city in the morning and return at night: The male population

> is sucked into the City at daybreak, and scattered again as darkness falls. It finds itself towards evening in its own territory in the miles and miles of little red houses in little silent streets, in number defying imagination. Each boasts its pleasant drawing-room, its bow-window, its little front garden, its high-sounding title—'Acacia Villa' or 'Camperdown Lodge'—attesting unconquered human aspiration.[72]

Because most men built houses to suit their individual needs and to impress others, suburbs grew in an unplanned, haphazard way. However, the exceptions were the few planned suburbs like Bedford Park on the western edge of London. Hilary and Mary Evans describe it:

> An enterprising landowner and the well-known architect Norman Shaw conceived, planned and created an estate comprising houses which for their day were attractive as well as functional, together with a clubhouse,

The London suburb Bedford Park, an attractive community with the space, privacy, trees, and gardens that the Victorian middle class valued.

inn and co-operative stores, all in a setting of trees and gardens.[73]

A magazine article of the time described it as "the prettiest and pleasantest townlet in England . . . a Utopia in brick and paint."[74] The middle class wanted houses with locked gates for privacy and space in quiet, attractive neighborhoods with parks and trees.

A Victorian house was likely to be a scaled-down version of the stately homes of aristocrats with decorative turrets and towers and belfries. An upper-middle-class family might afford a ten-room house with six bedrooms, a bath with running water, a dining room, a drawing room, and a library. Before the front door a carriage drive curved from the street and back. Most of these drives, however, had no function since few middle-class families could afford to keep a carriage, an undertaking that also required outlays for buying, feeding, and shoeing a horse, and paying a driver or groom.

Inside, Victorians filled their rooms with heavy, carved furniture, covered their walls with elaborately patterned wallpaper, and placed decorative objects and knickknacks in all available spaces. Women lounged in drawing rooms furnished with plush flowered carpets; men gathered in dark-paneled libraries with heavily carved furniture. Servants lived in unheated upper-level or attic rooms with few furnishings and did most of their work in dark kitchens and food cellars. Most Victorians bought ready-made furniture from catalogs and often selected pieces representing multiple period styles. They stuffed the rooms with furniture, but with little regard for the basics of interior decoration. One authority notes that "Grecian, Elizabethan, and Gothic furnishings might adorn different rooms in a single home, with occasional Japanese or Middle Eastern accents."[75] Wingfield-Stratford is outspoken in her criticism of Victorian taste:

> Victorians seemed to be fast losing both the desire and the capacity to surround themselves with beautiful things. Solidity and pretentiousness were the qualities chiefly aimed at. Everything in the house seemed to be playing a game of pretending to be something else. On the mantelpiece blossomed flowers of wax, in conservatories formed by hideous glass domes. The mirror, or the part of it that was not concealed by draperies, had become a garden for painted flowers.[76]

FEMALE CLOTHING SYMBOLIZES WEALTH

Victorian clothing, even more than housing, symbolized wealth and social status. Throughout the Victorian era, men dressed in suits, overcoats, and top hats, varying from time to time only in the style of collars, lapels, neckties, and hats. Female dress, on the other hand, varied greatly. New dyes added new colors; mills in factory cities provided numerous weaves in wool, silk, and cotton; and the sewing machine, invented in 1840, reduced the cost. Women wore hats and were corseted into long dresses displaying ruffles, bows, and embroidered ribbon. There were styles for special occasions, even for "stages of mourning."[77]

In their dress, women were expected to symbolize the family's wealth by means of conspicuous consumption, conspicuous leisure, and conspicuous waste. Wide crinoline skirts and costly fabrics served as obvious displays of wealth. Similarly, a woman advertised her leisurely role by wearing outfits she could not possibly work in, dresses with narrow hobble skirts and sleeves tightly fitted from elbow to wrist. To illustrate that her family had wealth enough to waste, she changed styles often and wore ruffles, bows, and bustles that could be maintained only by the labor of servants. Roberts says of the woman's role: "In becoming an expensive and accomplished decorative object, she functions as an advertisement for her husband's (or father's or lover's) economic potency and privileged position."[78]

THE ROLE OF WOMEN

The complex role assigned to middle-class women, symbolized by clothing, developed along with the concept of refinement.

An affluent woman and her daughter from the mid-1800s display the popular wide skirts and ruffles.

Refinement prescribed, on one hand, that women bring gentility to the middle-class family and, on the other hand, that women refrain from paid employment unless absolutely necessary. The notion that women should not work coincided with the time when men began to shift their workplace from home or farm to shops, factories, and offices. And since polite society frowned on women with jobs, marriage became the primary goal for the daughters of the middle class.

In *Victorian Working Women,* historian W. F. Neff writes, "To get ready for the marriage market a girl was trained like a racehorse. Her education consisted of showy accomplishments designed to ensnare young men."[79] Girls were trained in music, especially piano playing, to lure men to lean over them at the keyboard, allowing them a socially approved opportunity to be close together. As a display of refinement, they learned to draw and to speak French, taught by a governess in the home. Petrie says, "Needlework, drawing, and painting flowers were also considered good bait in the husband-fishing business."[80] Girls practiced every variety of needlework, an important diversion for their gatherings in the drawing room to pass their leisure time. Many made use of this time by embroidering altar cloths and items for church bazaars.

Girls also had to learn the proper attitudes and behavior regarding sex, and the rules were strictly controlled by men. Since women were totally dependent on men, they had to guard their reputations for male approval. One convention held that unmarried men and women were

Learning to play the piano was an important part of a Victorian girl's education.

never to be alone together unless they were engaged, and not always then. Another dictated that sexual experience be strictly confined to marriage. A sexual scandal, even a rumor of one, could destroy a woman's reputation. If a woman went in a carriage accompanied only by a man who was not her husband or a close male relative, her reputation was ruined, and she could not regain it. Even for a married woman, sexual pleasure was considered sinful; sexual experience was a duty either to her husband, for his pleasure, or to society, to achieve pregnancy, thereby increasing the population.

A middle-class woman once married had little choice but to try to please her husband. Above all she was to be subservient

MALES FOSTER FEMALE INCOMPETENCE

Victorian girls, directed to give their full attention to acquiring a husband, failed to learn practical skills. In The Victorians, *Charles Petrie blames Victorian men, who demanded that their women be innocent and ignorant.*

"The real tragedy was that although the Victorian girl was skilled in the art of acquiring a husband, she was, unlike her predecessors in earlier centuries, given no training of any sort in her practical duties as a wife, and this was the case even in many lower middle-class families. She was quite untrained in household management, and generally unable to control her servants. She had no idea of the value of money, and too often squandered what her husband gave her. Even in the very important matter of child-bearing she had to learn by experience with all the physical and psychological shocks which this implies.

The blame for this state of affairs largely rested with the Victorian male. Innocence was what he demanded from the girls of his class, and they must not only be innocent but also give the outward impression of being innocent. White muslin, typical of virginal purity, clothed many a heroine, with delicate shades of blue and pink next in popularity. The stamp of masculine approval was placed upon ignorance of the world, meekness, lack of opinions, general helplessness and weakness; in short, a recognition of female inferiority to the male."

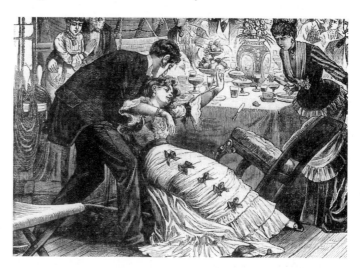

Victorian social norms dictated that women exhibit helplessness and fragility, sometimes through displays such as fainting.

to him—a devoted and submissive wife and the mother of his children. She was to preserve the home for her husband as a refuge from the harsh outside world. It was her job to be what her husband, and all other Victorian husbands, wanted her to be. Altick calls this stereotyping of women's personality "women's serfdom":

> She was to cultivate fragility, leaning always on the arm of the gentleman who walked with her in a country lane or escorted her in to dinner. The woman of the well-off middle class lived, in effect, under one of those capacious glass domes which protected parlor bric-a-brac—stuffed birds, ornate shells, papier-mache constructions, wax fruit and flowers—from dust.[81]

Training girls and women to play this role meant that they learned nothing about caring for a household or managing servants. Since every middle-class household had at least one servant and wealthier ones had more, women either had to manage secretly and still give the impression of idleness or let the servants manage as best they could.

Besides having no identity of her own, the Victorian woman had no rights. When she married, everything she had, even her clothes, became the property of her husband, and she lost all control over her possessions. By law, her husband had legal custody of the children, and until 1840 she could lose a dependent infant. Petrie says, "A husband had an absolute right over the person of his wife; he could lock her up, and he could compel her to return home if she ran away from him."[82] Until 1857, divorce was possible only by means of an act of Parliament introduced for an individual case. After 1857, a husband could divorce his wife on simple grounds of adultery, but a woman had to prove not only her husband's adultery but also an additional offense, such as desertion, cruelty, rape, or incest.

MEN, WOMEN, AND REALITY

The role imposed on Victorian women indirectly says much about the role of Victorian men. They were expected to be as manly, as virile, strong, and robust, as women were believed to be fragile. They were under great pressure from their peers to be fierce competitors at work, lords of their homes, and protectors of their wives and children. Moreover, their status and reputation depended on their ability to succeed, the measure of which was evident in the richness of their homes, their possessions, and their clothing.

Of course, not all middle-class families fulfilled the idealized model. Magazines, like *Punch*, constantly published cartoons mocking the henpecked husband and the domineering wife. In real day-to-day living, women had much more power than they appeared to have. By cleverly taking advantage of the assumption that they were frail creatures, ever submissive to male authority, they learned to manipulate their husbands in ways that gave them considerable control over their lives and the lives of their husbands.

FAMILY LIFE AND LEISURE

Middle-class Victorians emphasized the value of family togetherness and liked to portray themselves in the activities they shared. Though Victorians frequently conjure up the stern image of parents frowning on pleasure and fun, they in fact pursued numerous kinds of entertainment. Many activities involved visiting with friends in their homes. Groups gathered around the piano for singing. Children and sometimes whole families put on theatricals, those they had created or versions of popular plays. Their parties were more than sitting conversations with drinks. Victorians served elaborate dinners followed by dancing or parlor games like charades. In summer families gathered for croquet and lawn tennis. Middle-class families often sat around a table and listened to the father read novels aloud. The nineteenth century saw a remarkable growth in the number and popularity of novels, which were often published first in serial form in weekly magazines and then in three-volume book form.

The middle class suburban dwellers were close enough to the city to attend cultural events there. Stage plays ranged from Shakespeare to sentimental melodramas lavishly produced, as Hilary and Mary Evans explain:

Croquet was a favorite summer activity for middle-class families.

Londoners greet one another as they ride through Hyde Park, a fashionable place to socialize and show off their wealth and style.

Production styles tended toward the spectacular, as did those of pantomime; but while dramatic producers aimed at naturalistic representations of shipwrecks and horse-races, storms or the battle of Agincourt, pantomime spectacle reached its grand finale with magic transformation scenes which left reality as far behind as possible.[83]

Music halls featured ballad singers and operas, orchestras and oratorios. Lectures were popular as were author readings; Charles Dickens wore himself out fulfilling the demand for public readings of his novels.

Furthermore, middle-class Victorians participated in individual and team sports and gave rise to spectator sports as big business. They cycled and played cricket and tennis; football (soccer), however, they left to the working classes. They formed clubs where local players participated, and they formed special clubs to build teams that played in stadiums and charged admission. As spectators, they liked boxing, cricket, football, tennis, and walking matches, which were races in which men competed by walking fast, the only Victorian sport that has died out.

At the peak of middle-class prominence around 1850, the newly rich, proud materialists relished every opportunity to display their success. They promenaded on the fashionable streets and took carriage rides in Hyde Park, where they could see and be seen. Attending picnics, sporting events, and drawing-room dinners offered splendid opportunities to display their finery. The middle class had become the social trendsetters.

MIDDLE-CLASS MORALITY

At midcentury, the middle class, besides setting social standards, also assumed responsibility for establishing and enforcing moral standards. Middle-class Victorians made strict rules for themselves and tried to impose them on the upper and working classes. They vehemently asserted their ethics and morality because they believed that they had discerned the system God intended people to follow. Reader explains Victorian thinking:

> Moral standards, as the expressed will of God, could not be flouted without grave impiety: a point of view which emphasizes the element of authoritarianism in the Victorian outlook. From God downwards through the Queen and the established social order, there were those, it was generally held, whose place it was to give orders and those whose duty it was to obey. Obedience was one of the first of many duties exacted of a child by parents, and it was a virtue highly prized throughout society by those who considered they had a right to demand it.[84]

The middle class, investing its moral principles with the same importance accorded to God and the British Constitution, considered its exercise of authority a moral right.

The Victorian middle class never wavered in its belief in the sanctity of work. By means of work, a man could rise and hold an honorable position in society, and he could avoid the terrors of falling into ruin. Success by work necessarily required the disciplines of frugality, self-denial, dedication to one's appointed occupation, industry, honesty, and self-reliance. "Heaven helps those who help themselves" was their maxim. On the issue of work, middle-class Victorians practiced what they preached. The habits of railway builder George Stephenson illustrate the point.

> George Stephenson, at the height of his career, would be up at daybreak or before and would go on until well into the evening, riding, walking, inspecting, dictating (once, it is said, for twelve hours at a stretch, until his secretary almost fell off his seat with weariness), instructing his pupils ('you young fellows don't know what *wark* is'), trying to solve his problems as he lay in bed.[85]

On the issue of honesty, practice was less consistent. Many an employer saw fit to bend the rules for a good cause—his—but not for the cause of a worker or a subordinate, a practice that did not go unnoticed by workers.

The middle-class ideal of personal conduct can be summed up in the word "respectability," a value ranking almost as high as "work." The attributes of respectability included the standard Victorian qualities of "sobriety, thrift, cleanliness of person and tidiness of home, good man-

THE MORAL CODE IN REALITY

In Victorian England a number of Protestant sects existed outside the state-sponsored Church of England; their members were predominantly middle class and subscribed to the principles of hard work and strict moral behavior. Called Evangelicals, they acquired a reputation as work addicts, moral scolds, and hypocrites who harshly judged those who failed to follow their regimen of stern living yet were themselves guilty of moral faults. In *Victorian People and Ideas,* Richard Altick refutes this stereotype of Evangelicals. He says that for every Evangelical community that was preachy and foolish there was "another whose temperate and humane interpretation of the rules strikes us as reasonable and possibly even engaging. There were plenty of Evangelical families who laughed and played." He emphasizes that not every family tried to "suppress the notion of sex functions out of existence." Altick suggests that some families quietly tried to follow the Sabbath rules, such as the Ruskins, whose son John became a famous Victorian essayist and art critic. The Ruskins observed the Sabbath "by turning pictures to the wall, eating only cold meals (so that the servants would not have to desecrate the day by working), and devoting the long hours of enforced inactivity between church services to reading the Bible or religious papers." Altick suggests that the stereotype developed because extreme cases and fanatic behavior got more publicity, and they continue to receive attention "in popular histories of Victorian manners more prominently than their actual incidence warrants."

ners, respect for the law, honesty in business affairs, and, it need hardly be added, chastity."[86] Of those attributes, sobriety was especially important, and they preached temperance, which was then defined as total abstinence from drinking alcoholic beverages. Victorian middle classes were shocked at drunkenness, especially its prevalence in the lower classes. Without considering the circumstances facing the working poor, they ridiculed alcoholics as weaklings unwilling to resist temptation. Many in the middle class joined temperance organizations that urged others to sign pledges of abstinence. In 1888 one temperance organization, the Band of Hope, had nearly 1.5 million members pledged not to touch alcohol. The most radical teetotalers, as the nondrinkers were called, envisioned a temperance reformation, but, as historian

SAVING FALLEN WOMEN

On December 2, 1860, the London Observer *reported on a meeting of prostitutes called by clergymen. During the meeting, held at a restaurant after midnight, the clerics offered the women refreshments and sermons chastising their sins and fallen lives. Those who repented their ways were offered a safe place to stay, but the reporter does not explain what long-term offers the clergymen made.*

"A most interesting meeting took place on Wednesday morning (having commenced at midnight on Tuesday), at the St. James's Restaurant, St. James's Hall, in connection with the Great Social Evil. The meeting was one of fallen women, invited for the purpose of hearing prayer and admonitions. It was originated by gentlemen connected with the Country Towns Missions, the Monthly Tract Society, Female Air Society, London Female Preventive and Reformative Association, and other societies. . . . At least 250 persons were present, solely composed of the females of the class described, excepting nearly forty clergymen and gentlemen who had convened the assembly, no other male visitors being admitted. . . .

The Hon. and Rev. Baptist Noel then addressed the assembled in an eloquent, pathetic, and affectionate discourse, styling his hearers his 'dear young friends.' He then drew a contrast between the history of a virtuous woman from her childhood, and the position of those who have strayed from the path of virtue. He then assured his hearers that some of them might yet be happy, for they had a friend who was more tender than a mother and stronger in his love than a father, and who would never desert them—that friend was Jesus, their Saviour. . . .

Several of the fallen sisterhood buried their faces in their handkerchiefs and sobbed aloud, and more than one had to be removed in an almost unconscious condition from the room. It was announced that any present who repented their sins would be received into the London Reformatory or the Trinity House, and arrangements would be made and funds provided for their reception elsewhere. The meeting broke up at three o'clock a.m. The conduct of the females present was highly creditable and quite void of levity."

David M. Fahey explains, when they "demanded unfermented wine in the eucharist [Mass], traditionalists denounced them as troublemakers."[87]

Troublemakers of another sort were prostitutes, of whom there were a great many during the early years of Victoria's reign, when working-class women had only three major occupations—laundry, needlework, and domestic service. Since none of these paid enough to support one person, much less a family, women often supplemented their incomes by working as prostitutes. Many middle-class women joined organizations to stop the trade in sex or to rescue these "fallen women," but they met resistance from the girls who needed the money and the men who patronized them. Over the course of Victoria's reign, prostitution declined. The cause is uncertain: The work of organized middle-class women may have had an effect, or prostitution may simply have declined with the rise in workers' pay.

The moral code of respectable middle-class Victorians was supported by "two pillars." According to Wingfield-Stratford, they are "It pays to be good" and "If you must commit sins, at least don't talk about them."[88] By the first, one got ahead and by

Drunkenness was severely frowned upon by middle-class Victorians. Here, police officers escort drunks to court.

the second, one stayed ahead. Some critics thought the ideals of middle-class ethics and morality were set too high for human nature, resulting in hypocrisy—a difference between what people said they believed and what they actually did. Nonetheless, people's public behavior during Victoria's reign was more disciplined than before or after.

Middle-class Victorians, however, have been criticized for more than hypocrisy. They have been called anti-intellectual and spiritually empty because they too narrowly focused on work and money. Poet Matthew Arnold described mid-Victorian England "in the 'sick hurry' of modern life."[89] Others accused middle-class Victorians of self-righteousness for trying to impose their morals on the rest of society. Though many may have been shallow and narrow, their strength lay in their ambition and energy to build a new social and economic structure, in which reform was possible for themselves and those in the working classes below them.

Chapter
6 An Era of Political, Social, and Educational Reform

By the mid–nineteenth century the social and economic power attained by the middle class initiated an atmosphere ripe for reform. Though the middle classes needed little help economically, they wanted greater suffrage and more representation in Parliament. The upper classes fought to retain the power they had and, thus, resisted reform, but fear of violent revolution and the power of public opinion forced them to pass reforms in spite of their efforts. The working classes needed reforms of every kind and had neither political nor economic power to achieve them. Yet, during the second half of the nineteenth century, the upper classes passed many acts to improve the lives of working people. By 1850, the upper classes still controlled Parliament, and, fearing the growing wealth and influence of the middle class, made alliances with lower classes to balance the power of the middle class. The resulting coalition achieved favorable working-class reforms.

Political reform in Victorian England meant the development of democratic institutions and the weakening of the monarchy and aristocracy, which tradi-

tionally had held power. Many people considered such a major change destabilizing. English society was permeated with the belief that social standing carried authority with it, a notion embraced by the middle class and accepted even by the working classes, which would later obtain suffrage, increasing their stake in an orderly society. As reform bills passed, the Victorians had to face the problem of the common man, who was about to enter politics and culture. Altick says that "now it was the manual workers' turn. Bitterly though many might deplore the advent of democracy, somehow it had to be accepted as an accomplished fact."[90] Some worried that democracy was a leap in the dark; others feared that government would become radicalized. As late as the 1870s, "democracy" was still a dirty word to many people, including Queen Victoria, who did not like it. One of her biographers reports:

A *Democratic* Monarchy [she wrote to Earl Granville in 1880] . . . she will not *consent to belong to*. *Others* must be found, *if* that is to be, and she *thinks* we are on a dangerous and doubtful

The elaborate multistory Parliament Houses, home of the Victorian Parliament.

slope which may become too rapid for us to stop, when it is too late.[91]

Despite fears and anxiety, democracy did progress in Victorian England.

EXTENDING SUFFRAGE AND REFORMING GOVERNMENT

England progressed toward democracy by means of the three reform bills. The First Reform Bill of 1832, which passed after riots broke out throughout the country and did no more than add to the ranks of voters certain propertied members of the middle class, nevertheless opened up a trend. By 1865, Britons were determined to extend the franchise, and no government could survive without seriously addressing this demand. Thus, after years of maneuvering between the Whigs and the

Tories, Parliament passed the Second Reform Bill of 1867. This bill enfranchised the remainder of middle-class males and most male town workers, adding almost a million voters. Like the 1832 bill, this bill also related voting to property, but on terms more favorable to new voters: "This time the terms were so liberal that nearly all men who owned or rented town domiciles of any kind, including lodgers paying £10 or more a year, were covered."[92]

Two groups—agricultural workers and women—still could not vote. In 1884 the government headed by Prime Minister William Gladstone presented Parliament with a reform package that extended the vote to 2.5 million agricultural workers and allowed for locally elected governments in rural areas. Women writers and other female leaders had worked to have women included in the 1884 bill, but Gladstone refused. At the end of the century, democracy had advanced in some ways, stalled in others: Only 60 percent of males were registered to vote, and British women would not receive the vote until the twentieth century.

Extending the vote to include all classes was a major accomplishment, but the system also needed reforms to remove corrupt and unjust practices. Two practices kept the government in the hands of the upper classes. First, becoming an MP was prohibitively expensive for all but the very wealthy. Candidates often won elections by bribing voters and by treating them to food and drink. Second, people cast their ballots in public, where powerful candidates could watch the voting and intimidate the electorate. Prior to 1868, a committee of the House of Commons had reviewed petitions of candidates claiming that opponents had corrupted voters and that those who paid bribes routinely received favorable results. The Corrupt Practices Act of 1868, designed to eliminate the practice of buying votes, transferred all such petitions to the courts for an unbiased decision. The Ballot Act of 1872 adopted the secret ballot to protect voters from intimidation, and the Corrupt Practices Act of 1883 imposed strict limitations on campaign expenditures. After 1883, bribery and treating declined, as did the cost of filing petitions of corruption. Thus, as democracy was becoming more widespread, its machinery ran more fairly.

Not all the problems arising from industrialism and the growing, shifting population could be solved by giving the right to vote to greater numbers of people. Many problems required a reorganization of governing units. Before 1834 England had had no local government; safety and care of the poor were administered by local church parishes and town magistrates. The establishment of a Local Government

Liberal reformer William Gladstone served four nonconsecutive terms as prime minister from 1868 to 1894.

Board in 1871 began a trend toward local control of national affairs. Roads, bridges, and jails had to be built and maintained. Crowded cities needed sewage and clean water systems. The County Councils Act of 1888 set up sixty-one counties to be administered by elected administrators, and the Local Government Act of 1894 established rural and urban district councils to facilitate resolution of the differences in urban and rural problems. A National Board of Health managed all matters relating to health, such as water, sewage, and vaccination against disease. Control of education and relief for the destitute, however, remained in the hands of local municipal officials.

Workingpeople began to see better times in 1871 when the Trade Union Act granted legal status to unions, giving workers the right to organize, meet, and press for reforms. The unions had struggled since the 1830s for better wages and working conditions, but, because they lacked money and legitimacy in the eyes of Parliament and the public, their proposals for reform had met strong opposition. In the wake of the 1871 act, trade unions hired full-time leaders to foster good relations with employers and lobby for favorable legislation. Highlighting the change in the lot of the workers and their unions that had occurred by the end of the century, Altick observes "not only did almost

Much-needed improvements in sanitation, such as the construction of sewers (pictured), were implemented during the Victorian era.

all the workers have the vote but men from their own class were actually sitting in Parliament. They were curiosities but no longer absolute rarities. The old order had changed indeed, yielding place to new."[93]

PROTECTING WORKERS

As a result of political reforms, social reform became practically achievable. Social reform meant improved working and living conditions for the lower classes. Better working conditions came with new laws controlling the number of hours workers could work. Limited hours were set first for children and then for women. The dates of the Factory Acts illustrate the gradual improvement in working conditions. Factory Acts passed between 1819 and 1833 were ineffective because the laws failed to provide for inspectors to enforce the acts and fine violators. The Factory Act of 1833 prohibited the employment of children under the age of nine in textile mills and restricted children ages ten to twelve to an eight-hour day and a six-day week. This act broke new ground in several respects: It "provided for professional inspectors armed with the power to enter factories, examine the premises, and assess fines."[94] An 1842 act extended conditions of the child labor provisions of the 1833 act to workers in coal mines. The Children's Factory Act of 1844 restricted the number of hours children could work daily to six and a half and restricted women's hours to twelve. The Ten Hours Act of 1847

The passage of new labor laws gradually improved the lot of working children.

shortened hours for all women and children in factories and mines (but not in small shops) to ten, at which point men also benefited. Because women and children did jobs that were essential to the running of many factories and mines, owners shut down their operations after ten hours, and the men's workday was therefore reduced as well. The act passed in 1850 granted all workers a half-day off on Saturday.

In 1878 Parliament consolidated the patchwork of Factory Acts into one and granted inspectors wider power to enforce the laws. Historian Dennis J. Mitchell identifies further improvement: "Subsequent acts added to the list of dangerous industries, established specific regulations, and permitted the appointment of women as factory inspectors."[95] A Factory Act in 1901 "absolutely" forbade the employment of children in all factories and workshops. Over a seventy-year period, working families acquired more time for themselves and more safety in their workplaces.

ATTACKING POVERTY AND FILTH

Social reform in the workplace indeed helped the working classes, but the dismal conditions of their daily lives, especially those of unskilled workers, also needed reform. Throughout the Victorian period, poverty at the level of utter destitution was an acute social ill. There were multiple causes: low wages, unemployment, personal circumstances like alcohol abuse and large families, illness, death of the wage earner, and old age. Poverty fluctuated with the economy, but even in good times, people already poor lived in dread of total impoverishment. Reader explains:

> Poverty lay at the root of working-class life and had a powerful influence on the ways of life and habits of thought of the whole new race of town-bred working men. Even when they found themselves more or less securely above the line of want, they did not easily shake off a dread of falling back into the slough they had climbed out of.[96]

Only two government reforms made any attempt to alleviate poverty. Workhouses had for years offered food and shelter to orphans, widows, and old and sick people; the revised Poor Laws of 1834 grudgingly extended relief to the unemployed poor, but benefits were so meager that while they perhaps prevented starvation, they certainly did not eliminate poverty. Yet this was the only government program to aid impoverished Britons until the twentieth century. The other reform was the repeal of the Corn Laws, which had resulted in bread prices so high that in 1840 this dietary staple took between a quarter and a third of the income of unskilled workers. In 1846 the Corn Laws were temporarily repealed and in 1848 permanently repealed. The price of bread came down and helped workers for a time, but at the end of the nineteenth century, estimates indicate that a third of the people still lived in poverty.

Hunger is not necessarily obvious to an observer, but death by disease and squalid, filthy living conditions are; consequently, Parliament more readily passed reforms to improve those conditions. Edwin Chadwick's 1842 *Report on the Sanitary Conditions of the Labouring Population* had aroused concern over the conditions of the poor and generated enthusiasm for reform and social legislation. Because of his thorough study, the next thirty years saw improvements in vaccination, sanitation, water, housing, and air quality.

The Vaccination Act of 1840, which was government's response to epidemics between 1837 and 1840, provided for free smallpox vaccinations to the poor. In 1853 vaccinations were made compulsory, but opponents resented being forced to submit to the invasive procedure and claimed the vaccine had not been proved safe or effective. Despite improvements to the vaccine, opposition persisted, and before the end of the century laws had to be modified to allow people to refuse in some cases. Historian James Hill says, "The cherished principle of individual rights had prevailed against the legislated imperatives of public health."[97]

PUBLIC WORKS: WASTE REMOVAL, CLEAN WATER, AND CLEAN AIR

The Public Health Act of 1848 set about the task of cleaning up the cities and providing clean water, a task so huge it required both new laws and administrative reform. The act created a central General Board of Health to safeguard the population. Historian Rosa Lynn B. Pinkus explains the complexity of the problem:

> The tasks before the General Board of Health were unprecedented, and involved years of basic development in statistical collection, map making and engineering as well as legal, administrative, and financial innovation. Before sewers could be built, for example, precise geological maps had to be drawn and experiments undertaken with various clays, pipe sizes, and levels to achieve maximum velocity of flow. Although the General Board of Health was a failure to the extent that it lacked powers of compulsion and excluded London, it made the first steps toward completing an enormous task.[98]

London was added to the list of places required to provide sewer and water systems when the Metropolitan Board of Works was established in 1855.

Under the supervision of Metropolitan Board's chief engineer, Joseph Bazalgette, nicknamed "the sewer king," engineers devised a scheme for improving London's drainage and waste removal. The scheme involved large trunk sewers running along either side of the Thames River and carrying waste to points well below the city into the tidal estuary. Large pumping engines maintained the flow in these sewers. Built between 1858 and 1865, the system comprised thirteen hundred miles of sewage pipes and used over three hundred million bricks. Similar systems were

Engineer Joseph Bazalgette oversaw London's drainage and waste removal renovations.

then built in other cities. Not until the last quarter of the nineteenth century did cities begin treating sewage instead of dumping raw waste into the rivers.

As engineers built sewers, other engineers devised a scheme to bring clean drinking water to the city. The clean-water scheme involved building great reservoirs in the upland districts to collect fresh water and then pipe it to city centers. Once clean water was available, cities built public baths and houses for washing clothes and removed the tax on soap. Volunteer organizations supplemented government action. Pinkus explains some of the volunteers' work: "Sanitary questions were frequently discussed in journals; the Ladies' Sanitary Association distributed soap and disinfecting powder and educated women about washing clothes, covering food against flies, and proper nutrition of infants."[99] As a result of these measures taken to remove sewage and provide clean water and soap, cholera epidemics were eliminated.

Four public health acts passed in 1858, 1866, 1872, and 1875 all concerned administration of the health laws. The country was divided into districts and regional and local boards were established to carry out sanitation and water laws. At each stage in building this administrative plan, Parliament incorporated provisions giving power to inspectors to see that cities complied with the laws. The final act in 1875 consolidated and amended all of the previous acts related to public health.

Chadwick's report had also pointed out the additional problems of polluted air and overcrowded housing. Acts passed in the 1860s and 1870s forced factories to reduce the amount of soot from coal-burning furnaces and forced chemical plants to reduce the noxious fumes escaping from their chimneys. Measures to effect cleanup of inside air coincided with the acts aimed at cleaning up outside air. Factories were required to provide better ventilation for their workers, and housing codes incorporated by-laws requiring better construction. Though the poorest of the working class still lived in one- or two-room back-to-back units, new laws required that low-income housing be constructed with better materials and better systems of ventilation.

SAFE STREETS AND A RISING STANDARD OF LIVING

Government also addressed the problem of public safety. Unguarded dark streets in communities overcrowded with poor people had been rife with crime. First, gas lighting was installed. It brightened the major streets in London, which were lit nightly by nearly four hundred lamplighters employed by the city. As additional street lighting was installed in residential areas, crime in the city declined.

Further contributing to safety and the reduction of crime was the introduction of professional police forces. In 1835 the Municipal Corporations Bill enabled towns to establish police forces, but people at first resisted this change, preferring to depend on the local night watchman. In 1856 legislation created an Inspector of Constabulary with the power to enforce a standard of police protection. Gradually, as the protection afforded by trained police officers became apparent, the public attitude changed. Consequently, London's force grew from approximately eighty-five hundred in 1868 to fifteen thousand in 1886, and its lighted streets became safer.

Like the political and social reforms that occurred during Victoria's reign, the improvements in public safety offered certain obvious benefits. How much these helped the working classes has been difficult for historians to measure, as Newsome notes:

The extent to which a rising standard of living was enjoyed by all classes of society has been the subject of much debate among social and economic historians. On the whole recent research, especially that based on analysis of consumption expenditure within the working classes has established that living standards were rising gradually from the middle years of the century, and that lower-income segments shared in the economic growth.[100]

What is clear is that political and social reforms were not enough for the expanding

Once a hotbed of crime, London's streets became safer with the addition of gaslights.

POLICE AND CRIME

In the first excerpt, from The Victorians: At Home and at Work, *Hilary and Mary Evans explain why citizens initially resisted the presence of paid police forces in their communities. In the second excerpt, published in* Victorian Britain: An Encyclopedia, *historian Don Richard Cox identifies one of London's most notorious criminals who terrorized unpoliced areas.*

"Then as now, the police were seen as lackeys of the establishment, more concerned to safeguard the interests of the propertied classes than to apprehend wrongdoers and bring them to justice. They were also accused of devoting more time to catching unmuzzled dogs than to protecting the citizens—there were parts of London where police scarcely dared to venture even in pairs; during crime epidemics like that of Jack the Ripper, the inhabitants of these unpoliced areas formed their own corps of vigilantes. Nevertheless, the amount of crime substantially diminished as the number of police increased."

* * * * *

"In the autumn of 1888 the murder of several prostitutes in London's East End galvanized the city. The killer, also known as the Whitechapel murderer, cut the throats of his victims, disemboweling and viciously mutilating the corpses. The savagery of the killings, as well as taunting notes sent to the police and signed 'Jack the Ripper' (one accompanied by part of a victim's kidney) made the crimes a national scandal. Scotland Yard's inability to apprehend a killer added to the Ripper's legend, which became the subject of newspaper articles, songs, and stories."

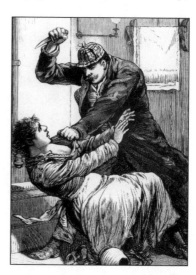

A depiction of Jack the Ripper in one of his notorious slashing attacks that terrorized London in 1888.

industry and growing democracy. The society also needed educational reforms.

REFORMING CHILDREN'S EDUCATION

Education in England in the early nineteenth century had declined from its past levels. In Shakespeare's day England had a national system of elementary schools for young children and high schools, called grammar schools, with a rigorous curriculum taught by qualified teachers. During the first half of Victoria's reign, there were very few elementary and grammar schools open to the general public, and a boy could become an adult without having received any formal education. Education was in disarray because in these rapidly changing times groups disagreed: Industrialists wanted literacy and arithmetic taught; humanitarians wanted an education in classics; and politicians squabbled over government control, curriculum, teaching methods, and the place of religion in school.

Nevertheless, institutions of elementary education, run by charitable or religious groups, were available in most villages and towns. Schools operated by the Ragged School Union provided free education until 1870. In rural areas "dame" schools, taught by a neighborhood woman in her home, provided instruction in elementary reading and crafts. The Anglicans, the Roman Catholics, and Protestant sects separated from the Church of England each ran their own schools. Middle-class parents could pay to send their children to private schools, and upper-class children were taught at home by governesses or tutors. All of these arrangements were privately controlled; there was no standard curriculum and no compulsory attendance policy.

Secondary education was in equal disarray. Working-class children above age twelve almost never attended school. Secondary education was available to middle-class boys in proprietary schools, which were boarding schools run for profit and notorious for poor food and flogging. Alternatively, a middle-class boy might board with an Anglican clergyman, who tutored a few boys to supplement his income. The upper classes sent boys to high-cost academies, called public schools, like Eton and Rugby, which prepared them for the university. For girls, a few small boarding schools were available, offering "drawing, music, French, and other 'accomplishments' to girls of the upper middle class."[101] By 1860, when the middle class pressured Parliament for secondary education, a commission recommended a three-tiered system to prepare students for the university, for business and industry, or for skilled labor.

In 1870 Parliament passed the Elementary Education Act, directing the establishment of national elementary schools available to all children in England and Wales. The government supplied the necessary money for teachers' salaries and buildings where facilities were lacking or failed to meet government standards. In many places, poorer children attended the new national schools, and children of the affluent continued to attend private or religious schools. By 1880 attendance was compulsory to the age of ten. Historian David Hopkinson reports on the growing urgency for education: "There was by 1890 a widespread conviction that a democratic political system in a modern industrial and trading society must be backed by a much better educated people."[102] An act of 1876 had granted three additional years of free education to all children who passed a standard examination at age ten. This act led to the organization of a central secondary school for those who wished to continue their education to age fifteen. In 1899 Parliament passed a law making school compulsory to age twelve and created the Board of Education, with a president who was the national minister for all education up to the university level.

Oxford University, the oldest institution of higher learning in England. Traditionally an all-male school, Oxford began to admit women in the nineteenth century.

REFORMING POSTSECONDARY EDUCATION

As business and industry became ever more complex, workers needed a variety of new skills, and training was not available in the existing postsecondary institutions. Traditionally, higher education meant Cambridge and Oxford, universities that were available to upper-class boys belonging to the Church of England and educated in preparatory schools. Change came when the two universities opened their doors first to boys from other Christian denominations and later to women. These traditional universities educated students in classical languages, philosophy, mathematics, and literature.

But new institutions were needed to offer instruction in new subjects. The University of London was the first to be established and offered, besides the traditional subjects, instruction in sciences and modern languages. Within the next thirty years, a dozen new universities opened in Birmingham, Exeter, Liverpool, and other cities around England. While all of these offered a traditional curriculum, they also stressed sciences, and some added colleges of medicine with teaching hospitals. Cambridge and Oxford added degrees in law and history, and its professors taught extension classes in London emphasizing science and engineering. Between 1870 and 1890 at least six colleges, with an academic curriculum comparable to other universities', opened for women. With the growth of universities, Britain again achieved a "position of educational eminence in the sciences,"[103] with an emphasis on biology, physics, history, and language.

New institutions were also needed to provide technical education, but this kind of education lagged behind both secondary and university reforms. For sons of middle-class industrialists, for clerks, shopworkers, and skilled workers and artisans, mechanics institutes finally became available. In 1883, for example, the Finsbury Technical Institute opened to train workers in technological studies. Gradually evening classes, some in basic literacy and arithmetic, became available to working adults who needed either to supplement a poor childhood education or to retrain for the demands of new jobs. Though educational opportunities at all levels increased during the second half of the nineteenth century, historians observe that by the end of Victoria's reign, "the lack of a systematic education program and the misunderstanding of technical education's role had resulted in a serious decline in British industry and technology."[104]

LITERACY AND READING

In a society in which the demand for education exceeded the availability of schools, books and newspapers flourished. Striving Victorians eager to improve themselves exalted books as symbols of civilization. Altick explains the coincidental demand for

THE PENNY DREADFUL

In The Printed Image and the Transformation of Popular Culture, *Patricia Anderson explains the sensational content and graphic illustrations of the Victorian fiction called "the penny dreadful."*

"The stories contained in examples of this type of small, inexpensive, paper-bound book invariably tended to dwell lovingly on crime, horror, and the seamier side of relations between the sexes. So, naturally they attracted a substantial following of people in search of pleasurable terror, revulsion, titillation, and general escapism. After all, who but the most dedicatedly serious-minded reader could fail to respond to the lure of titles such as *Ada, the Betrayed, or, The Murder at the Old Smithy, The Apparition, Crimes of the Aristocracy, The Secret of the Grey Turret, The Death Ship, or, The Pirate's Bride*, and *Varney, the Vampyre*, also published as *The Feast of Blood?*

An illustration from an 1847 edition of this last work provides as good an example as any of the kind of imagery that attracted readers with a penny to spend and a taste for the dreadful. Prominent in the centre of the composition is a horrifically bony and toothy vampire (Varney without doubt) whose lips are fastened on to the neck of a young female victim who flails her arms in agony. As she tormentedly arches her back, she thrusts her breasts upwards, thus providing Varney with a convenient place to rest a loving hand while he takes his nourishment. Here indeed was what our expert on 'cheap literature' called a '*pièce de résistance* [outstanding item] for the strong stomach of the million.' Astute publishers of such illustrated fiction were well aware of the popular appetite for graphic images of violence and horror."

books and the technological advancements to produce them cheaply:

> The expansion of the reading public was accompanied—it is impossible to distinguish cause from effect here— by technological advances which made the printed word both cheaper

and more readily accessible than it had ever been before. The steam press, the stereotyping process, new papermaking machinery and the adoption of cheaper ingredients than the former staple of rags, machinery for prefabricating bindings, and, late in the century, mechanized typesetting enabled books, magazines, and newspapers to take their place among the other Victorian commodities that were cheapened by mass production and made more widely available by energetic merchandising. By the end of the century English publishing had undergone a revolution.[105]

This vast increase in print publication could not have taken place, however, without a corresponding increase in a literate reading public.

Historian Monika Brown suggests that Victorian readers fall into two categories: "'respectable' readers ranging from the well-educated elite to ambitious working people, and the 'mass' public."[106] Serialized novels appealed to both categories of readers, especially the novels of Charles Dickens, which often appeared in weekly magazines, a chapter at a time, for months. In addition, respectable readers sought information and education in religion, politics, and analysis of social issues; publications describing the latest advances in science were particularly popular. Toward the end of the century, specialized magazines appeared on, for example, travel, sport, and theater. The mass readership liked entertainment provided in escapist fiction with criminals and rogues as characters, improbable plots, and reckless heroes. From street vendors, they bought broadsides about current events and royal gossip, true crime stories, and little books on history, humor, and heroes. In a society without television or radio and with the challenge of a changing way of life, Victorians had a great desire to escape in reading or to learn from it, and writers and publishers accommodated them.

The cover of a compilation of Charles Dickens's novelettes. The author's humorous commentaries on Victorian society were extremely popular.

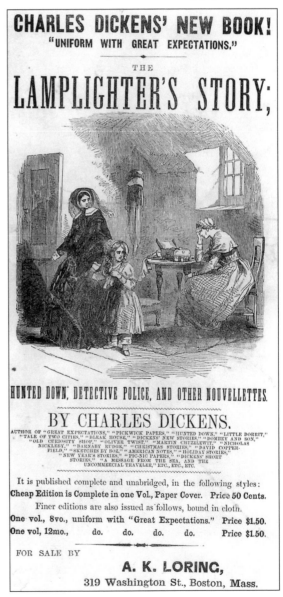

The rising number of readers and the abundance of available reading materials symbolize, in a way, the great reforms that took place in Victorian England. Political, social, and educational reforms freed many, especially those in the working class, from isolation and allowed them to feel part of the whole society. Behind these visible changes, however, there existed a quiet, stable group of scholars who provided the theory and scientific research that made many of these changes possible.

7 The Importance of Science

The popularity of science information published in magazines and the numerous additions of science and science-related curricula to British education underscore the important role science played in Victorian England. Discoveries in theoretical science formed the basis on which medical and practical science progressed. Most importantly, the methods used by scientists were completely transformed.

The word *science,* as we know it today, acquired its meaning during the Victorian period. Prior to that time, those who studied nature were called "natural philosophers," and they reasoned logically about observable phenomena of nature. Victorian scientists developed systematic methods of observation, conducted experiments, and drew conclusions. With the increased use of the scientific method came greater specialization and the emergence of distinct academic disciplines, like physics and chemistry. These fields, in turn, became further specialized as organic and inorganic chemistry, and so on.

For years England had had many amateur scientists who regularly gathered data and recorded their findings, but there were few professional scientists. Those professionals who did exist were poorly paid and drew little respect from the community. Altick says, "Most professional scientists were men of private initiative; those who were university members seldom taught their subjects. Endowed, organized research began only in the wake of the reforms, which swept Oxford and Cambridge between 1850 and 1860."[107] Moreover, scientists carried on a running debate over which was more important—theoretical or practical, or applied, science. All science was hindered by inadequate education. Altick highlights the problems:

> Until the middle of the century . . ., except in non-Anglican or secular schools for boys of the commercial middle class, very little provision was made for scientific study in the schools or universities. Critics pointed out that such instruction as there was failed to take into account the discoveries of the past three centuries.[108]

But scientists overcame problems, and, particularly in the second half of the century, made important contributions.

Advances in Theoretical Science

Theoretical scientists made important contributions in a variety of fields. Geology was popular and at the cutting edge of fieldwork and fossil research. In 1830 leading geologist Charles Lyell published *Principles of Geology,* in which he reported that layers of rock formations spanned immense periods of time and concluded that the earth was likely formed around a billion years ago—startling news to Victorians. Lyell's interest in the past inspired scientists to study archaeology and develop a new field, anthropology, which

Resistance to Change

The kind of conservative thinking that resisted changes in medical practices applied also to changes in industrial advancements. In Our Fathers, *Alan Bott describes the resistance to the automobile.*

"The cause of the motor car suffered most in England from Sleepy Hollow reactionaries. A tricycle driven by an internal combustion engine, with benzoline vapour exploded by an electric spark inside its one cylinder, was built in London in 1885, when Gottlieb Daimler and others in France had already begun to use internal combustion for 'horseless carriages.' It was at once ruled that the new tricycles and the newer auto-carriage came under an Act of 1865, whereby vehicles dependent upon engines had been forbidden a speed of more than four miles an hour, and must be preceded by a man carrying a red flag to warn drivers [of horse-powered carriages]. England's hands were tied for ten years by this kind of crassness, while France and Germany developed the motor car. The first automobile race, between Paris and Rouen, was hardly mentioned by the English press except as a matter for ridicule. Even when the fantastic restriction was removed in 1896, early motor cars were jeered at, abused for the dust they raised and the horses they terrified, and condemned for their danger. Drivers were said to be daring fools who were certain of death if they kept to their rash hobby; and in the procession of cars from London to Brighton, to celebrate the end of the red-flag law, each of the high, blunt contraptions that broke down met hoots of laughter and dislike. As a result of all this, France was allowed to dominate the market in motor cars."

focused on the physical and cultural evolution of early peoples. Chemistry, which had never been taught in secondary schools before 1850, lagged behind, however, because students lacked research training. A few working chemists contributed new information to atomic theory and deduced the existence of electrons, even though these tiny particles could not be observed under a microscope. British mathematicians contributed new methods in algebra and new systems of statistics that made sophisticated analysis of social and health data possible. According to historian Paul Theerman, "Physics was a Victorian invention. From natural philosophy and rational mechanics, . . . the physicists of the nineteenth century wove a new synthesis, applying sophisticated mathematical methods to the study of light, heat, sound, electricity, and magnetism."[109] In biology, scientists developed a new theory of cell structure and conducted the investigations that culminated in the theory of evolution, versions of which were published almost simultaneously by Charles Darwin and Alfred Russel Wallace.

Publications by two scientists, Charles Lyell and Charles Darwin, instigated greater controversy than any other scientific study of the period. When Lyell reported that the earth was about a billion years old, he contradicted what many Victorians accepted as truth—that an unchanging universe had been created by God about six thousand years ago. Some were able to reconcile their belief with the new information by reasoning that God, after all, might have created the universe in long stages rather than all at once. Many Victorians, however, accepted Lyell's evidence because it was based on scientific investigation.

Charles Darwin's report on evolution, published as *On the Origin of Species by Means of Natural Selection* in 1859, dealt a harsher blow to traditional thinking. Darwin found evidence that species change by the process he called natural selection, that only the strongest, or best adapted, individuals survive, while those unequal to the struggle die out, and that new physical characteristics, advantageous to organisms in given environments, evolve over time—assertions that are still being investigated at the beginning of the twenty-first century. Nonetheless, the mass of evidence

Scottish geologist Charles Lyell determined that the earth was about a billion years old.

Charles Darwin's theory of evolution contradicted the prevailing belief that humans were created by God.

compiled by Darwin presented a persuasive case that all forms of life arose from primitive forms and continued to evolve by natural selection. The editors of *British Literature* imagine the effect this information had on devout Victorian believers:

> One can vaguely imagine the explosion which this theory set off. In one terrible blow it seemed to destroy the traditional conceptions of man, of nature, and of the origin of religion and mortality; and to substitute for each an interpretation that was deeply distressing. Man was reduced to an animal, the descendant of apes. Nature, which had been the witness of a divine and beneficent God and a source of moral elevation, became a battlefield in which individuals and species alike fought for their lives, and the victor was the best, not morally but physically, the toughest and the roughest and the quickest on the kill.[110]

The public response to these reports, widely publicized and discussed in the newspapers and periodicals, varied. The working classes, lacking enough education to grasp the argument or its significance, easily shrugged off the news but enjoyed the cartoonists, who satirized Darwin. The attention of the middle class was diverted by hard work. It was the Christian clergy and the intellectuals who struggled, trying to reconcile the scientists' findings with their traditional interpretations of Scripture. Being well educated, they could see the validity of the scientific methods used by Lyell and Darwin, and they were open-minded in their analysis of the newly presented data.

ADVANCES IN MEDICAL SCIENCE

Using the same rigorous methods of observation and experimentation, scientists made major breakthroughs in medical science. Acceptance, however, was delayed because influential people clung to old ideas. One old idea was the miasma theory of disease, put forth by Chadwick and others in connection with the cholera epidemics. Belief in this theory led officials to remove stinking filth from crowded city streets and, thus, improved health in some ways. But raw sewage from the streets was dumped into rivers, the source of drinking water, contributing to cholera epidemics in 1848 and 1864.

The experimental work of several British scientists had already confirmed the bacterial theory of disease put forth by French chemist Louis Pasteur. Numerous proofs that microorganisms, not noxious odors, cause disease were convincing to much of the scientific community. Many respected professionals refused to accept the findings, however, characterizing as quackery claims that a single primitive organism could cause a specific disease. British surgeon Joseph Lister, who applied bacterial theory to the practice of his profession, confirmed in careful experiments the relationship between microorganisms and surgical wound infections. The logical conclusion from his findings was that wounds should be kept free from bacteria by thoroughly cleansing operating rooms and performing all hospital procedures under sterile conditions. Lister published his results in 1867, but his recommendations, called the "antiseptic method," did not become common practice in surgery until 1893, largely because a very influential doctor, who still believed in the miasma theory, refused to implement Lister's methods. During the 1890s, use of antiseptic methods—"steam sterilization of linens, boiling of instruments, systematic scrubbing, and the donning of surgical gloves, caps, gowns, and ultimately masks"[111] gradually became standard practice.

The adoption of two other medical breakthroughs also was held up by conservative adherence to old beliefs. First, the use of anesthesia in surgery and childbirth began in America in the 1840s and the news quickly spread to England. Doctors first used ether, but obstetrician James Simpson turned to chloroform because ether caused irritation in the nasal passages and throat. Historian Loralee Macpike reports that use of anesthesia met with considerable opposition on religious grounds from those who believed that pain in childbirth was "divinely ordained and therefore necessary."[112]

However, after Queen Victoria allowed her physician to administer chloroform when she went into labor before the birth of her eighth child in 1853, the public accepted its use.

The second scientific advance that encountered popular resistance was the use in experimental medicine of anesthetized animals. Conservative religious groups objected because they felt with animal experimentation that scientists were trying to know too much and were infringing on divine knowledge. Others objected simply because they believed the practice was inhumane and might lead to experiments on humans.

By the last decade of the nineteenth century, opposition to the germ theory of disease, the use of anesthesia, and the use of animals in medical experiments had been largely overcome, and new practices in medicine and new methods of experi-

Joseph Lister, shown here at a patient's bedside, put forth his "antiseptic method" in 1867, but it was not widely practiced until the end of the century.

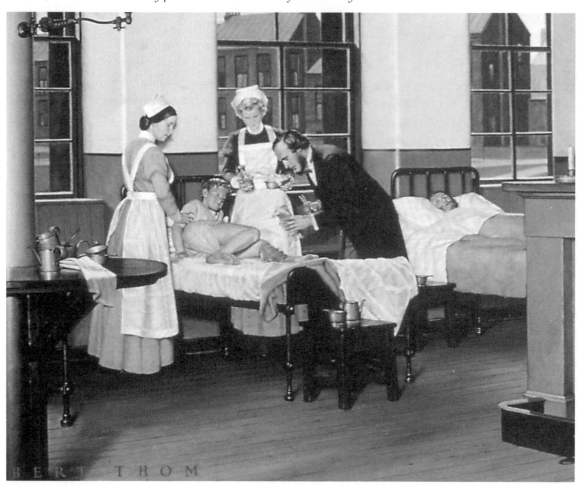

Medical Advances: From Open Windows to Brain Surgery

In the first excerpt, from Notes on Nursing, *Florence Nightingale, the founder of modern nursing, reflects on the notion of "night air" and recommends sleeping with an open window. In the second excerpt, from* Victorian Britain: An Encyclopedia, *Sally Mitchell gives an account of new surgical procedures accomplished after the introduction of anesthesia.*

"Another extraordinary fallacy is the dread of night air. What air can we breathe at night but night air? The choice is between pure night air from without or foul night air from within. Most people prefer the latter. An unaccountable choice. What will they say if it is proved to be true that fully one-half of all the disease we suffer from is occasioned by people sleeping with their windows shut? An open window most nights in the year can never hurt any one."

* * * * *

"By the last two decades of the Victorian era, surgeons dared to open the thorax, the abdomen, and even the skull. Cesarean section was no longer performed only to snatch the infant of a woman already dead or dying, but gave some hope of saving both mother and child. Advances in surgical pathology provided materials for improved diagnosis. Skin grafts, colostomies [surgery of the colon], repair of congenital orthopedic defects such as clubfoot, removal of ovarian cysts, excision of cancers in the digestive tract, and appendectomies entered the repertoire of surgical procedures. The French physiologists who mapped the brain's functions made it possible to localize tumors and abscesses within the skull, although the death rate was much higher in brain surgery than in other fields. Surgeons were using X-ray photographs to locate foreign objects in the body and examine broken bones within months after their discovery was published in [the journal] *Lancet* in 1896."

mentation thrived from then on. Many other medical successes followed the invention of new instruments and equipment designed by newly trained engineers and manufactured in new English industries.

Advances in Engineering and Technology

England's successful industry depended on the integration of theoretical science with the practical sciences of engineering and technology. During the first half of the nineteenth century, these three disciplines often operated separately, but during the second half the complexity of industry required that they work together. Altick says of the early development of technology:

> Although in some fields practical applications necessarily lagged far behind theory, technology had already constructed ample proofs of science's benefit to mankind. In fact, the national genius for empiricism had produced a race of inventors a century in advance of the pure scientists such as [physicists] James Clerk-Maxwell and John Tyndall who were to come into prominence during Victoria's reign. It was native technology which had made Britain the birthplace of the industrial revolution, with all the benefits that it implied.[113]

It was indeed the integration of the sciences in later years that gave English industry the means to reach its peak in the 1870s.

Theoretical science provided the underpinnings on which the applied sciences developed. For example, knowledge of thermodynamics, the physics that deals with the relationships of heat and other forms of energy, was necessary for building high-pressure steam engines for trains and factories. Knowledge of the properties of electricity was necessary for the invention of new methods of light and power. Knowledge of organic chemistry was necessary to invent artificial dyes, synthetic textiles, plastics, and high-

powered explosives. To extract metals from ore and make durable alloys for machines, scientists needed to know metallurgy. Engineers used both physics and mathematics in designing machines and metal products for the market.

As the century wore on and scientists became more specialized, many advances became possible. Theoretical scientists provided knowledge, and engineers and technologists made machines and products a reality. Nowhere was their work more evident than at the Great Exhibition of 1851. Historian Phillip Thurmond Smith says of the exhibition, "The machinery gallery was the noisiest and most popular, where visitors could see huge marine engines, locomotives, hydraulic presses, reapers, and the like. An electric telegraph was installed inside, which was connected with Edinburgh and Manchester."[114]

Victorians were proud of the accomplishments of British scientists, visible in the country, the city, homes, and shops. They had built railway trains and steamships. Engineers had designed a railway system with tunnels, arched bridges, and terminals that were architectural marvels. English clothes were the products of spinning, weaving, lace, and sewing machines. Workers operated steam hammers and lathes. Doctors employed microscopes, gynecological forceps, and X rays. Citizens rode bicycles and, after Rudolf Diesel refined the internal combustion engine, they could think of owning a car. Office workers had typewriters and adding machines, and everyone could look forward to living in electrically lighted houses in the near future. Kitchens could be equipped with eggbeaters, scales, scissors, coathooks, and bottles. As Anthony Wood sums up, "The list is endless, and one invention following upon another

Visitors admire the machinery at the Crystal Palace's Great Exhibition, the showcase of Victorian innovations.

VICTORIANS ACCUSED OF BAD TASTE

The Victorians have long had a reputation for terrible taste in decorating, among other things. In For Queen and Country, *Margaret Drabble elaborates on design expert Nikolaus Pevsner's opinion of objects displayed at the Exhibition of 1851.*

"'The aesthetic quality of the products was abominable.' These are hard words. [Pevsner] goes on to argue that designers had not yet learned to cope with the newly invented processes of production, such as machine weaving and electro-plating, and were applying the wrong techniques to the wrong materials. Certainly some of the objects indicate more pride in the fact that a thing *can* be done than interest in the use or beauty of the finished object—take, for example, the wonderful knife with eighty blades and other instruments, made by Rodgers and Sons of Sheffield. It was heavily decorated with gold inlay, etching and engraving—a remarkable piece of work, but neither use nor ornament. The Osler fountain of cut crystal glass was famed more for its size and weight than for its beauty; it weighed four tons. Designs for carpets and fabrics show, as Pevsner points out, a lack of restraint, a lack of plan, a picking from here and there of jumbled scraps of pattern, a confused eclecticism. Eclecticism is a word one cannot avoid long when talking about the Victorians, for it so perfectly describes their attitude to decoration; it is the art of borrowing from various sources to suit oneself. The Victorians had a great deal to be eclectic about; easier travel and the spreading Empire, as well as new techniques, provided a vast range of new patterns—peacocks from India, carpet designs from Turkey and Persia, lace designs from France, even sphinxes from Egypt. The Victorian instinct was not to look for uniformity of style, but to jumble everything up together, at random."

only confirmed the average Victorian in his belief that all was for the best in this unprecedented age of progress."[115]

By the end of the century scientific thinking dominated intellectual thought. In the early decades of the Victorian period natural science had connections with other areas of thought, such as theology and philosophy, but by the end of the century science was the model for judging other subjects. In 1870 Norman Lockyer, the editor of the magazine *Nature*, predicted that in the future the average person would be "made to feel that Science dogs him at every footstep, meets him at every turn, and twines itself round his life."[116] Lockyer's prediction turned out to be correct.

England at the End of an Era

When Queen Victoria died in 1901, England was indeed a vastly different society from what it was at the beginning of her reign. Over the course of Victoria's reign, England had become a world power. Major institutions had been transformed. And most people had, over the course of the period, attained a more safe, more prosperous, and more convenient urban life. Victorians were proud of their accomplishments, but a little of their early optimism had begun to fade.

England could pride itself on accommodating great change peacefully. The empire had grown to cover one-fourth of the world's land and include one-fourth of the world's people. The country survived tremendous population growth. Droves of people left the countryside and settled in cities, and by the end of the era most of them had achieved better housing, a cleaner environment, and a safer community. The government, once firmly controlled by royalty and wealthy aristocrats, had become a democracy in the hands of all classes of people. The traditional class system was broken of its rigidity, and a more open class system offered opportunities to those who wanted to rise and more compassionate attitudes toward those who could not. Industry had changed all elements of society—from transport by railway to whipping eggs with an eggbeater. These changes had taken place gradually without violence. Historian Walter E. Houghton reflects:

> In 1858 a Victorian critic, searching for an epithet to describe "this remarkable period in which our own lot is cast," did not call it the age of democracy or industry or science, nor of earnestness or optimism. The one distinguishing fact about the time was "that we are living in *an age of transition.*" This is the basic and almost universal conception of the period.[117]

THE DECLINE OF INDUSTRY

By the end of the century, however, England's industrial power was declining. Having reached its peak in the 1870s, England was losing ground to other industrializing nations. England had pioneered the factory system, and Germany and America had learned from England and gradually overtaken British industry. Wingfield-Stratford notes:

By the end of the century signs were apparent that the long period of Victorian prosperity was drawing to a close, that the curve of real wages had touched its highest point. Rival powers were at last beginning to bring their full resources into play, and England would have need of all her energy and imagination if she were to maintain her supply of those goods from abroad that were necessary to her existence.[118]

No single cause explains the decline, but historians have suggested several related contributing factors.

Historians have identified blind spots and faults in Victorian thinking, common human oversights rather than malicious or deliberate fallacies. When their business and industry grew and prospered so markedly, Victorians tended to be too optimistic, believing their good times were destined to go on and on. They were not alert to possibilities of what could go wrong and were not prepared for troubles. Moreover, many Victorians, often influential ones, resisted change and consequently hampered advancements when they were needed; for example, many resisted the railway and the automobile and others clung to outmoded theories of medicine. Late in the century, it became clear that early Victorians had placed too much faith in the laissez-faire

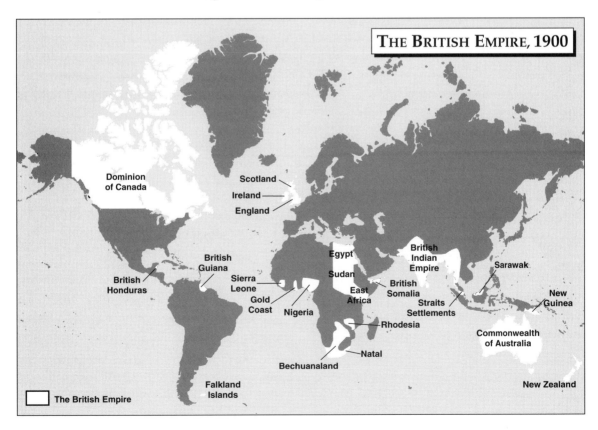

THE BRITISH EMPIRE, 1900

Dominion of Canada

Scotland
Ireland
England

British Guiana

British Honduras

Sierra Leone

Gold Coast

Nigeria

Egypt

Sudan

East Africa

British Indian Empire

British Somalia

Straits Settlements

Rhodesia

Sarawak

New Guinea

Commonwealth of Australia

Natal

Bechuanaland

Falkland Islands

New Zealand

The British Empire

REFLECTIONS AT THE END OF VICTORIA'S REIGN

In Victorian England: Portrait of an Age, *G. M. Young quotes an article from the* Times *of January 23, 1901. In it the writer evaluates what needs to be improved and what has been gained.*

There is much in what we see around us that we may easily and rightly wish to see improved. The *laudator temporis acti* [person who praises the past] may even contend that we have lost some things that had better been preserved. But no permissible deductions can obscure the fact that the period in question has been one of intellectual upheaval, of enormous social and economic progress, and, upon the whole, of moral and spiritual improvement. It is also true, unfortunately, that the impetus has to some extent spent itself. At the close of the reign we are finding ourselves somewhat less secure of our position than we could desire, and somewhat less abreast of the problems of the age than we ought to be, considering the initial advantages we secured. The "condition of England question" does not present itself in so formidable a shape as at the beginning of the reign, but it does arouse the attention of those who try to look a little ahead of current business. Others have learned our lessons and bettered our instructions while we have been too easily content to rely upon the methods which were effective a generation ago. In this way the Victorian age is defined at its end as well as at its beginning. The command of natural forces that made us great and rich has been superseded by newer discoveries and methods, and we have to open what may be called a new chapter. But "the first of the new" in our race's story beats "the last of the old." If we now enter upon our work in a spirit embodied in the untiring vigilance and the perpetual openness of mind that distinguished the QUEEN, if, like her, we reverence knowledge and hold duty imperfectly discharged until we have brought all attainable knowledge to bear upon its performance, her descendants will witness advances not less important than that of her long and glorious reign.

notion that if left alone, free of government interference, things would automatically improve. This mindset was especially prevalent in education and science. Wingfield-Stratford comments:

> The fathers of the Industrial Revolution were eminently practical men, workmen for the most part, of slender education, but with a great fund of native commonsense. But as time went on, machinery became too elaborate and complex to yield its secrets to men guided only by the experience of the workshop. It was the trained mathematician or research worker, deeply versed in the theory of his subject, to whom the future of invention belonged.[119]

England had waited too long to educate its workforce and encourage and train its scientists. When the government finally did get involved, it was too late to prevent Germany and America from overtaking British industry.

Economic historian P. L. Payne suggests that continuation of the economic supremacy England achieved in the 1870s could not have been sustained. England is a small island nation with limited resources and limited home markets and a limited share of the export market. When industry declined, England responded by expanding its services instead. According to Payne:

> For the British economy, then as now, the future lay in services. At the dawn of the twentieth century, Britain con-

Queen Victoria led her country through sweeping changes that provided a better life for many of her subjects.

tinued to lead in shipping, insurance, brokerage and commission services and in international banking and the supply of capital. Britain may have lost her leading position as an industrial power by 1901, but she remained the world's chief financial and trading power. This was no mean achievement.[120]

Nor were democratic reforms, the example of hard work, and a century of peace mean achievements.

Notes

Introduction: The Transformation of a Society

1. Anthony Wood, *Nineteenth Century Britain, 1815–1914*. New York: David McKay, 1960, p. 96.

2. Quoted in Walter E. Houghton, *The Victorian Frame of Mind, 1830–1870*. New Haven, CT: Yale University Press, 1957, p. 1.

3. Hilary and Mary Evans, *The Victorians: At Home and at Work*. New York: Arco, 1973, pp. 7–8.

4. Quoted in Evans, *The Victorians*, p. 33.

Chapter 1: The Queen and Her Role

5. Dorothy Marshall, *The Life and Times of Victoria*. London: Weidenfeld and Nicolson, 1972, pp. 31–32.

6. Marshall, *The Life and Times of Victoria*, p. 39.

7. Marshall, *The Life and Times of Victoria*, p. 40.

8. Marshall, *The Life and Times of Victoria*, pp. 56–57.

9. Quoted in Marshall, *The Life and Times of Victoria*, p. 69.

10. Quoted in Marshall, *The Life and Times of Victoria*, p. 70.

11. Marshall, *The Life and Times of Victoria*, p. 144.

12. Marshall, *The Life and Times of Victoria*, pp. 154–55.

13. Quoted in Tamie Watters, "Albert, Prince Consort," in Sally Mitchell, ed., *Victorian Britain: An Encyclopedia*. New York: Garland, 1988, p. 17.

14. Quoted in Marshall, *The Life and Times of Victoria*, p. 159.

15. Quoted in Marshall, *The Life and Times of Victoria*, p. 120.

16. Sally Mitchell and James D. Startt, "Empire and Imperialism," in Mitchell, *Victorian Britain*, p. 263.

17. Quoted in Marshall, *The Life and Times of Victoria*, p. 214.

Chapter 2: England at the Beginning of Victoria's Reign

18. Quoted in David Newsome, *The Victorian World Picture*. New Brunswick, NJ: Rutgers University Press, 1997, pp. 133–34.

19. Richard Altick, *Victorian People and Ideas*. New York: W. W. Norton, 1973, p. 34.

20. Altick, *Victorian People and Ideas*, p. 21.

21. Sidney Johnson, "Aristocracy and Gentry," in Mitchell, *Victorian Britain*, p. 38.

22. Altick, *Victorian People and Ideas*, p. 35.

23. David Hopkinson, "Class," in Mitchell, *Victorian Britain*, p. 169.

24. T. Walter Wallbank and Alastair M. Taylor, *Civilization: Past and Present*, rev. ed., vol. 2. Chicago: Scott, Foresman, 1949, p. 162.

25. Wallbank and Taylor, *Civilization*, p. 65.

26. Wilson J. Hoffman, "Factories," in Mitchell, *Victorian Britain*, p. 280.

27. Newsome, *The Victorian World Picture*, p. 3.

Chapter 3: The Impact of Industrialization and Population Growth on Country and City

28. Newsome, *The Victorian World Picture*, p. 20.

29. Quoted in Newsome, *The Victorian World Picture*, p. 15.

30. Quoted in Altick, *Victorian People and Ideas*, p. 75.

31. Altick, *Victorian People and Ideas*, p. 45.

32. Altick, *Victorian People and Ideas*, pp. 36–37.

33. Quoted in W. J. Reader, *Victorian England*. New York: G. P. Putnam's Sons, 1973, pp. 67–68.

34. Altick, *Victorian People and Ideas*, p. 43.

35. Charles Dickens, *Hard Times*. 1854. Reprint, New York: New American Library of World Literature, 1963, pp. 30–31.

36. Reader, *Victorian England*, p. 105.

37. Bernard A. Cook, "Mining and Miners," in Mitchell, *Victorian Britain*, pp. 507–508.

38. Quoted in Newsome, *The Victorian World Picture*, p. 22.

39. Quoted in Reader, *Victorian England*, p. 113.

40. Quoted in Reader, *Victorian England*, p. 99.

41. W. John Smith, "London," in Mitchell, *Victorian Britain*, p. 465.

42. Quoted in Reader, *Victorian England*, p. 103.

43. Evans, *The Victorians*, p. 31.

44. Reader, *Victorian England*, p. 107.

45. Quoted in Reader, *Victorian England*, p. 107.

46. Altick, *Victorian People and Ideas*, p. 48.

47. Reader, *Victorian England*, p. 122.

48. Harry Schalck, "Suburbs and Planned Communities," in Mitchell, *Victorian Britain*, pp. 766–67.

Chapter 4: Poverty, Protests, and Politicians

49. Mark Neuman, "Poor Law," in Mitchell, *Victorian England*, p. 613.

50. Newsome, *The Victorian World Picture*, p. 18.

51. Reader, *Victorian England*, p. 98.

52. Esmé Wingfield-Stratford, *Those Earnest Victorians*. William Morrow, 1930, p. 85.

53. Altick, *Victorian People and Ideas*, p. 129.

54. Quoted in Newsome, *The Victorian World Picture*, p. 42.

55. Newsome, *The Victorian World Picture*, p. 44.

56. Newsome, *The Victorian World Picture*, p. 47.

57. Hazelton Spencer et al., eds., *British Literature: 1800 to the Present*, 3rd ed., vol. 2. Lexington, MA: D. C. Heath, 1974, p. 424.

58. Quoted in Spencer, *British Literature*, p. 412.

59. Quoted in Spencer, *British Literature*, pp. 485–86.

60. Quoted in Bernard D. Grebanier et al., *English Literature and Its Backgrounds*, rev. ed., vol. 2, *From the Forerunners of Romanticism to the Present*. New York: Dryden, 1949, p. 547.

61. Joseph Kestner, "Social Problem Novel," in Mitchell, *Victorian Britain*, p. 732.

62. Steven N. Craig, "Trade Unions," in Mitchell, *Victorian Britain*, p. 811.

63. Angus Hawkins, "Whig Party," in Mitchell, *Victorian Britain*, p. 856.

64. Quoted in Robert S. Fraser, "Robert Peel," in Mitchell, *Victorian Britain*, p. 586.

65. Eugene L. Rasor, "Pressure Groups," in Mitchell, *Victorian Britain*, pp. 635–36.

Chapter 5: The Rise of the Middle Class

66. Altick, *Victorian People and Ideas*, p. 19.

67. Reader, *Victorian England*, p. 172.

68. Quoted in Wingfield-Stratford, *Those Earnest Victorians*, p. 145.

69. Wingfield-Stratford, *Those Earnest Victorians*, pp. 45–46.

70. Wingfield-Stratford, *Those Earnest Victorians*, pp. 49–50.

71. Elizabeth Burton, *The Pageant of Early Victorian England, 1837–1861*. New York: Charles Scribner's Sons, 1972, p. 10.

72. Quoted in Charles Petrie, *The Victorians*. New York: Longmans, Green, 1961, p. 30.

73. Evans, *The Victorians*, p. 27.

74. Quoted in Evans, *The Victorians*, pp. 27–28.

75. Julia M. Gergits, "Home Furnishings and Decoration," in Mitchell, *Victorian Britain*, p. 368.

76. Wingfield-Stratford, *Those Earnest Victorians*, p. 224.

77. Helene Roberts, "Clothing and Fashion," in Mitchell, *Victorian Britain*, pp. 173–74.

78. Roberts, "Clothing and Fashion," p. 175.

79. Quoted in Petrie, *The Victorians*, p. 200.

80. Petrie, *The Victorians*, p. 205.

81. Altick, *Victorian People and Ideas*, p. 53.

82. Petrie, *The Victorians*, p. 207.

83. Evans, *The Victorians*, p. 67.

84. Reader, *Victorian England*, p. 21.

85. Reader, *Victorian England*, p. 183.

86. Altick, *Victorian People and Ideas*, p. 175.

87. David M. Fahey, "Temperance Movement," in Mitchell, *Victorian Britain*, p. 789.

88. Wingfield-Stratford, *Those Earnest Victorians*, p. 149.

89. Quoted in Altick, *Victorian People and Ideas*, p. 97.

Chapter Six: An Era of Political, Social, and Educational Reform

90. Altick, *Victorian People and Ideas*, p. 14.

91. Quoted in Newsome, *The Victorian World Picture*, p. 235.

92. Altick, *Victorian People and Ideas*, p. 134.

93. Altick, *Victorian People and Ideas*, p. 95.

94. Dennis J. Mitchell, "Factory Acts," in Mitchell, *Victorian Britain*, p. 282.

95. Mitchell, "Factory Acts," p. 282.

96. Reader, *Victorian England*, pp. 98–99.

97. James Hill, "Vaccination and Smallpox," in Mitchell, *Victorian Britain*, p. 833.

98. Rosa Lynn B. Pinkus, "Public Health," in Mitchell, *Victorian Britain*, p. 649.

99. Pinkus, "Public Health," p. 650.

100. Newsome, *The Victorian World Picture*, p. 26.

101. David Hopkinson, "Secondary Education," in Mitchell, *Victorian Britain*, p. 245.

102. Hopkinson, "Secondary Education," p. 247.

103. George Mariz, "Higher Education," in Mitchell, *Victorian Britain*, p. 245.

104. Alan Rauch, "Technical Education," in Mitchell, *Victorian Britain*, p. 248.

105. Altick, *Victorian People and Ideas*, pp. 64–65.

106. Monika Brown, "Literacy and the Reading Public," in Mitchell, *Victorian Britain*, p. 456.

Chapter 7: The Importance of Science

107. Altick, *Victorian People and Ideas*, pp. 259–60.

108. Altick, *Victorian People and Ideas*, p. 259.

109. Paul Theerman, "Physics," in Mitchell, *Victorian Britain*, p. 601.

110. Spencer, *British Literature*, p. 419.

111. Sally Mitchell, "Surgery and Surgeons," in Mitchell, *Victorian Britain*, p. 775.

112. Loralee Macpike, "Childbirth," in Mitchell, *Victorian Britain*, p. 139.

113. Altick, *Victorian People and Ideas*, p. 107.

114. Phillip Thurmond Smith, "Exhibition of 1851," in Mitchell, *Victorian Britain*, p. 277.

115. Wood, *Nineteenth Century Britain*, p. 334.

116. Quoted in Richard R. Yeo, "Science," in Mitchell, *Victorian Britain*, p. 696.

Epilogue: England at the End of an Era

117. Walter E. Houghton, "Character of the Age," in Richard A. Levine, ed., *Backgrounds to Victorian Literature*. San Francisco: Chandler, 1967, p. 15.

118. Wingfield-Stratford, *Those Earnest Victorians*, p. 331.

119. Wingfield-Stratford, *Those Earnest Victorians*, p. 320.

120. P. L. Payne, "The British Economy: Growth and Structural Change," in Christopher Haigh, ed., *The Cambridge Historical Encyclopedia of Great Britain and Ireland*. London: Cambridge University Press, 1985, p. 275.

For Further Reading

James Truslow Adams, *Empire on the Seven Seas: The British Empire 1784–1939*. New York: Charles Scribner's Sons, 1940. A history explaining the growth and expansion of the empire, its importance to the British economy, and changes following Victoria's reign.

Hector Bolitho, *The Reign of Queen Victoria*. New York: Macmillan, 1948. A biography depicting the queen and her times.

Alan Bott, ed., *Our Mothers: A Cavalcade in Pictures, Quotations and Description of Late Victorian Women, 1870–1900*. An entertaining presentation of Victorian women in the late Victorian period.

Arthur Bryant, *Pageant of England 1840–1940*. New York: Harper and Brothers, 1941. A narrative of important elements of Victoria's reign and the events that followed.

John W. Deery, *A Short History of Nineteenth-Century England*. London: Blandford Press, 1963. An account of key social changes and political reforms of the century.

Lydia Farmer, *A Book of Famous Queens*. New rev. ed. New York: Thomas Y. Crowell, 1964. A collection of biographies of queens, including Queen Victoria.

W. D. Hussey, *British History 1815–1839*. Cambridge, England: Cambridge University Press, 1971. A history of the developments leading up to Victoria's reign and their effects still felt after her reign.

G. E. Mingay, ed., *The Victorian Countryside*. Vol. 1. New York: Routledge & Kegan Paul, 1981. Short essays on a variety of rural topics, such as land, country towns, and laboring life, accompanied by abundant photographs.

Daniel Pool, *What Jane Austen Ate and Charles Dickens Knew: From Fox Hunting to Whist—The Facts of Daily Life in Nineteenth-Century England*. New York: Simon and Schuster, 1993. An entertaining, detailed, insightful presentation of mundane Victorian life.

Margorie Quennell and C. H. B. Quennell, *A History of Everyday Things in England: The Rise of Industrialism 1733–1851*. London: B. T. Batsford, 1934. A history of common items used in Victorian households illustrated with black-and-white drawings.

———, *A History of Everyday Things in England 1851–1914*. London: B. T. Batsford, 1934. A companion volume, similarly illustrated.

Stanley Weintraub, *Victoria: An Intimate Biography*. New York: Truman Talley Books, 1987. A biography providing insight into the personality of the queen and some of the difficulties and triumphs she experienced.

Diane Yancey, *Life in Charles Dickens's England*. San Diego: Lucent Books, 1999. Offers a vivid glimpse of life in early Victorian England.

Works Consulted

Richard Altick, *Victorian People and Ideas.* New York: W. W. Norton, 1973. A colorful commentary on individuals, events, and philosophical ideas.

Patricia Anderson, *The Printed Image and the Transformation of Popular Culture.* New York: Oxford University Press, 1991. An illustrated account of the development of mass culture at a time of a growing reading public.

Edith C. Batho and Bonamy Dobree, *The Victorians and After, 1830–1914.* London: Cresset Press, 1958. An analysis of the effects of Victorianism, including, for example, the views of contemporary critics.

Alan Bott, *Our Fathers.* London: Heinemann, 1931. An analysis of the social customs of the late Victorian period.

Asa Briggs, *The Age of Improvement.* London: Longmans, Green, 1959. An analysis of improvements in Britain from the late 1700s through the Victorian era with an emphasis on economics, politics, and social reform.

Elizabeth Burton, *The Pageant of Early Victorian England, 1837–1861.* New York: Charles Scribner's Sons, 1972. A scholarly account of the middle-class rise to power.

Charles Dickens, *Hard Times.* 1854. Reprint, New York: New American Library of World Literature, 1963. A social-problem novel focusing on the evils of the factory and education systems.

John W. Dodds, *The Age of Paradox: A Biography of England, 1841–1851.* New York: Rinehart, 1952. An analysis of conflicting issues prevalent during the class conflicts of the 1840s.

Margaret Drabble, *For Queen and Country.* New York: Seabury Press, 1978. A survey of social and cultural history with an emphasis on the arts.

Hilary and Mary Evans, *The Victorians: At Home and at Work.* New York: Arco, 1973. An illustrated narrative covering, for example, work, leisure, and health.

Bernard D. Grebanier et al., *English Literature and Its Backgrounds.* Rev. ed. Vol. 2, *From the Forerunners of Romanticism to the Present.* New York: Dryden, 1949. A college literature anthology with extensive essays on the history of each period.

Christopher Haigh, ed., *The Cambridge Historical Encyclopedia of Great Britain and Ireland.* London: Cambridge University Press, 1985. A survey with an eight-part section on Victorian government, society, and culture.

Walter E. Houghton, *The Victorian Frame of Mind, 1830–1870.* New Haven, CT: Yale University Press, 1957. A scholarly analysis of the Victorian mindset on religion, politics, art, and economics.

Paul Kennedy, *The Rise and Fall of the Great Powers: Economic Change and*

Military Conflict from 1500 to 2000. New York: Random House, 1987. An analysis of how and why great nations throughout the world gained power and lost it again.

William S. Knickerbocker, "Victorian Education and the Idea of Culture," in Joseph E. Baker, ed., *The Reinterpretation of Victorian Literature.* Princeton, NJ: Princeton University Press, 1950. An analysis of the conflicting issues that made educational reform slow and difficult.

Richard A. Levine, ed., *Backgrounds to Victorian Literature.* San Francisco: Chandler, 1967. A collection of essays by scholars who discuss the major intellectual topics of the period, such as religion, art, science, and economics.

Dorothy Marshall, *The Life and Times of Victoria.* London: Weidenfeld and Nicolson, 1972. A biography describing the personal life of the queen, her family, and the government ministers she favored.

Marion Miliband, ed., *The* Observer *of the Nineteenth Century, 1791–1901.* London: Longmans, 1966. A collection of articles from the *Observer* newspaper, capturing the flavor of the times.

Sally Mitchell, *Daily Life in Victorian England.* Westport, CT: Greenwood, 1996. An account of issues that affected the day-to-day living of Victorians, such as public health.

———, ed., *Victorian Britain: An Encyclopedia.* New York: Garland, 1988. A thorough collection of essays covering people, events, and issues, written by historians.

Venetia Murray, *An Elegant Madness: High Society in Regency England.* New York: Viking, 1998. An entertaining account of the manners and tastes of the aristocracy just prior to Victoria's reign.

David Newsome, *The Victorian World Picture.* New Brunswick, NJ: Rutgers University Press, 1997. An analysis of social, political, and literary issues, each chapter taking a different perspective.

Florence Nightingale, *Notes on Nursing: What It Is and What It Is Not.* New York: D. Appleton, 1860. A practical guide to good health, written in a conversational style, covering such topics as "taking food," "beds and bedding," and "cleanliness of rooms and walls."

Charles Petrie, *The Victorians.* New York: Longmans, Green, 1961. The author attempts to depict the reality of Victorian conditions and to dispel distortions and stereotypes of the middle class.

E. Royston Pike, *"Golden Times": Human Documents of the Victorian Age.* New York: Frederick A. Praeger, 1967. A collection of documents written during Victorian times, chosen to present the human side of ordinary people.

Philip Priestley, *Victorian Prison Lives: English Prison Biography, 1830–1914.* London: Methuen, 1985. A description of prison life based on biographies of ordinary prisoners and prison records.

W. J. Reader, *Victorian England*. New York: G. P. Putnam's Sons, 1973. An illustrated history focusing on English social classes, especially the working classes.

Samuel Smiles, *The Life of George Stephenson, Railway Engineer*. Columbus, OH: Follett, Foster, 1859. A resume of the railway system and its results.

Hazelton Spencer et al., eds., *British Literature: 1800 to the Present*. 3rd ed. Vol. 2. Lexington, MA: D. C. Heath, 1974. A college literature anthology with extensive essays on historical background for each period.

Herbert L. Sussman, *Victorians and the Machine: The Literary Response to Technology*. Cambridge, MA: Harvard University Press, 1968. A scholarly investigation into the effects of and attitudes toward machinery.

Dorothy Thompson, *Queen Victoria: The Woman, the Monarch, and the People*. New York: Pantheon Books, 1990. A fresh appraisal of the personality of the queen, her work with political leaders, and her relationship with her subjects.

George Macaulay Trevelyan, *British History in the Nineteenth Century*. London: Longmans, 1924. A standard history on the period with emphasis on government and politicians.

T. Walter Wallbank and Alastair M. Taylor, *Civilization: Past and Present*. Rev. ed. Vol. 2. Chicago: Scott, Foresman, 1949. A survey of world history, scholarly and well written.

Esmé Wingfield-Stratford, *Those Earnest Victorians*. William Morrow, 1930. A personal, often opinionated, account of the middle decades of Victoria's reign.

Anthony Wood, *Nineteenth Century Britain, 1815–1914*. New York: David McKay, 1960. A scholarly history focusing on political, economic, and military issues.

G. M. Young, *Victorian England: Portrait of an Age*. New York: Oxford University Press, 1964. An extended essay searching for the meaning of "Victorianism," its religion and its politics.

Index

Picture Credits

Cover Photo: Popperphoto/Archive Photos

Archive Photos, 57, 61, 85

© Bettmann/Corbis, 31, 92

© Corbis, 77

Culver Pictures, 11, 18, 21, 30, 42, 52, 54, 69, 89, 91, 94

Dickens House Museum, 41

© Historical Picture Archive/Corbis, 70

© Hulton-Deutsch Collection/Corbis, 35, 72, 73, 84, 86

Library of Congress, 97, 102

North Wind Picture Archives, 33, 38, 46, 74

Photofest, 62

Prints Old and Rare, 14, 15, 17

Popperfoto/Archive Photos, 22

Snark/Art Resource, NY, 43, 45

© Stock Montage, 16, 27, 29, 67, 76, 81, 87, 101, 107, 113

About the Author

Clarice Swisher is a freelance writer and editor and a former English teacher. She taught English in Minnesota for several years before devoting full time to writing. She is the author or editor of more than twenty books, including *The Importance of Pablo Picasso*, *The Glorious Revolution*, and *Genetic Engineering*, published by Lucent Books, and *The Spread of Islam*, *William Faulkner*, and *John F. Kennedy*, published by Greenhaven Press. She lives in Saint Paul, Minnesota.